NILINA'S SONG

NILINA'S SONG

The Life of Naina Devi

AshaRani Mathur

NIYOGI
BOOKS

Published by
NIYOGI BOOKS
Block D, Building No. 77,
Okhla Industrial Area, Phase-I,
New Delhi-110 020, INDIA
Tel: 91-11-26816301, 26818960
Email: niyogibooks@gmail.com
Website: www.niyogibooksindia.com

Editor: K.E. Priyamvada
Design: Shraboni Roy

ISBN: 978-93-86906-07-6
Publication: 2017

Printed at: Niyogi Offset Pvt. Ltd., New Delhi, India

To

Nina
Courageous mother, friend and mentor
whose compelling life's journey is truly inspirational.

To Sharda Rao, whose hand of friendship and persuasion
led her back to music, an integral part of her being;

and to Sumitra Charat Ram, whose recognition
of Nina's musicality and organizational ability
reinforced her belief that the cultural landscape
was where she now belonged—
as Naina Devi,
artiste and patron.

Contents

Foreword..........9

Acknowledgements..........11

Introduction..........13

Nilina Sen
Calcutta: 1917–1935..........19

Rani Nina Ripjit Singh
Simla, Rajanagar, Delhi, Awadh: 1935–1953..........67

Naina Devi
Delhi: 1953–1993..........137

Epilogue
A Tribute to my Grandmother by Chandrajit Singh..........186

Paper 1: Women in Traditional Media
by Naina Devi..........189

Paper 2: Integration, a Heritage of the Performing Arts
by Naina Devi..........197

Endnotes..........202

Select Bibliography..........206

Text and Image Credits..........209

Index..........213

Foreword

The year 2017 marks the birth centenary of our mother, who passed away almost 25 years ago. Despite all these years we still feel her presence in so many ways. The love she gave us and the lessons she taught us through example, remain with us as a cherished inheritance.

A child of the Bengal Renaissance and granddaughter of the celebrated social reformer, Keshub Chandra Sen, she married an aristocrat of the Punjab. Traversing provinces, cultures and cuisines with aplomb, she soon became an accomplished hostess, wife and mother.

But alas, dark clouds appeared on the horizon and cast their shadows on her young life. Bereft and bereaved she navigated grief and loss with fortitude, donned the mantle of change and found her moorings in the performance arts, dedicating her life to music thereafter....

Nilina's Song: The Life of Naina Devi encapsulates the lives of Nilina, Nina and Naina. It rekindles memories of joy and sorrow and reaffirms our pride and privilege at having been nurtured by such a remarkable lady—our Mother. Courage was her credo. Accepting change of circumstance with dignity, breaking barriers of tradition with grace, she showed us the meaning of 'resilience' and 'resolve' and left an indelible imprint on our lives.

The interesting representation in the book of the social fabric of the time, the intellectual elite of Bengal, the aristocracy of Punjab, the landed gentry of Awadh and the cultural resurgence in the post-Independence era will enable readers to experience history. Naina Devi's passion for music, the bedrock of her existence, and the amazing trajectory of her life as artiste and patron will resonate with both young and old.

Nilika Rana

Acknowledgements

This recounting of Naina Devi's life was possible only because of the generosity of the many people who were interviewed and who shared their memories of a remarkable lady. I would like to thank them all; without these memories, this book could not have been written. What they told me has been woven into the text and is a large part of it.

First of all, my thanks to her children: Nilika, Rena, Ratanjit and Karanjit, better known to their friends as June, Billy, Reggie and Kenny, for their frank and open recollections including the painful periods of all their lives; and to her grandson, Chandrajit, or Baba, for his poignant account of her last days.

To her *shagirds* Vidya Rao and Shubha Mudgal—Vidya's own book on her guru, *Heart to Heart: Remembering Nainaji* was an invaluable source—who provided insights that can only come from the intimate nature of the teacher-student relationship. To Shobha Deepak Singh, who currently heads the Shriram Bharatiya Kala Kendra, for memories of her mother and the early days of the Kendra, and for recounting Naina Devi's role. To eminent Kathak dancers Uma Sharma and Shovana Narayan, for whom she was both mentor and friend.

And thanks also to all her friends and relatives who spoke to me, and the experts who guided me along the way: Raja sahib Suleiman of Mehmudabad, Pran Neville, Vinod Kapur, Saeed Naqvi, Vidya Shah, Lalita and Shaili Khanna, S. Kalidas, Partha Chatterji, Pradeep Rao and Dileep Rao.

My sincere thanks to the staff of the libraries at the India International Centre and the Nehru Memorial Museum and Library for their assistance in sourcing books. Last, but certainly not least, a special thank you to Samiha Grewal for all her work on transcribing the taped interviews.

— ASHARANI MATHUR

NAINA DEVI

27 September 1917 – 01 November 1993

Introduction

I first met Naina Devi barely two years before she passed away, but in the time that remained of her life we worked quite closely together on a series of albums for a well-known music label. We spent long hours with singers in recording studios, we often lunched at her home and occasionally went to concerts together. In that short time, Naina Devi became a mentor, from whom I learnt a lot about music, not so much in formal terms about its structures but in a more impressionistic way about its meaning and intent and emotion. As the seasons changed, the garden in front of her home was transformed into a coloured canvas where musicians would throng to celebrate *Chaiti* with hues of pink and *Basant* with deep yellow. It was there that I learnt, by listening, how seasons shaped the textures of music, its forms, its colours. She seemed to know every musician in Delhi and many of them would be present. Everybody was invited, her home was always open, always welcoming. They sang all the forms she loved, *thumri*, *chaiti* and *jhoola* and *kajri*, and *baramasa*, and after the music was over, everyone stayed on for dinner. '*Jab tak gaana, tab tak khaana*,' she would laughingly say, 'How can there be music where there is no bread broken together?'

Naina Devi was passionate about *thumri* and the only time that I was gently admonished was when I called *thumri* a genre of 'light classical music'. 'There is nothing light about it,' she said. 'It is a form that requires great skill and profound knowledge of classical music. The greatest *thumris* display and exact extraordinary "*taiyyari*", the skill born of years of practice, in their performance. You must appreciate and acknowledge the art and training behind the form,' she added. And though I had often heard qawwali singing, it was she who introduced me to the remarkable Ustad Jafar Hussain Khan sahib of Badaun whose performances combined the ecstasy of the devotional form with the polished musical training of the Rampur-Sahaswan gharana. At her insistence, Khan sahib and his group were recorded by the music label I worked for and that remained one of the most unique albums of the label: and, I am told, the only professional recording of this maestro made in India.

I say all this because although she has been gone for a long time, it is only now that I realize how little, in fact, I knew then about Naina Devi and who she really was. She would describe with great enthusiasm the features she produced for All India Radio and Doordarshan, and the interviews with musicians she conducted for telecast or broadcast; she would speak of the exhilaration of the early days of her work with the performing arts in Delhi; she would sometimes break into song to illustrate a musical point. She would delight in detailed explanations of the programmes she had conducted and how their themes expanded to draw in art forms of different kinds. Musicians would frequently congregate in her home and the conversation would sparkle with anecdotes, historical and contemporary, which offered rare insights into the world of Hindustani music and dance, through its most eminent artistes. Or discussions about some intricacy of technique or rendition which (regretfully) passed over my neophyte head, yet supplied the vocabulary which she would patiently and carefully explain to me later to add to my learning.

But she never spoke of her personal life. Of course I knew the bare facts—that she was widowed, that she had four children, that she had trained a number of students who became eminent singers and that she had a large group of friends and acquaintances both in the music world and out of it. I was completely ignorant of her connection with the royal house of Kapurthala. I had no idea that she was the aunt of Maharani Gayatri Devi of Jaipur whose grandmother, Maharani Suniti Devi of Cooch Behar, was Naina Devi's father's sister. Because her daughter's name was Rena Ripjit Singh, I assumed that she was from Punjab and found out only later that she was in fact Bengali, when she mentioned her sister Sadhona Bose, the dazzling star of the film *Raj Nartaki*. Still later I discovered the distinction and high standing of her natal family in Calcutta.

When I think about it, I wonder why this was so. Perhaps in that limited time, with so much focus on music, there was little opportunity to dwell on personal matters. Perhaps she thought I already knew, or had been told, about these things from others. Or perhaps it was just the delicate veiling of the private space that she kept for herself.

Rabindranath Tagore, always a prolific letter writer, was as keen an observer of human nature as he was of rural life; writing to a friend from Bolpur in the autumn of 1894, he remarked,

> 'We know people only in dotted outline, that is to say, with gaps in our knowledge which we have to fill in ourselves, as best we can...'

As I began work on this book, I realized that my 'dotted outline' was far sketchier than most, to say the least. To some extent, those 'gaps' were filled by the many stories recounted by her sons and daughters, her students, her friends, and all the people whose lives she had touched in many ways, who cherished her charm, her grace, her compassion. These recollections were invaluable. But the deepest unfolding of her life was like unravelling a skein that went backwards into a distant past well beyond her own past. The filling in of those dotted lines led to an exploration of the many environments that shaped her: social history and geography, the impact of family and its values, the heavy weight of that tradition, and her own personal and profound hunger for music and the performing arts. Much that makes us who we are is woven into our DNA as an inheritance from ancestors, and so it was with her. And so it remained until the very end, for she belonged to an earlier era when there was ample time to absorb and assimilate, and lessons lasted a lifetime.

What is more, it seemed to me that there was more than one woman who had occupied that specific time and space. This extraordinary life encompassed three different women—Nilina Sen, Rani Nina Ripjit Singh and Naina Devi—or

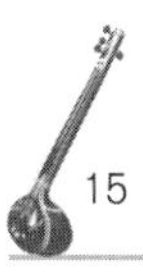

maybe just one woman who had shape-shifted into three avatars, reinventing and adapting herself to each phase she passed through. We live with imperatives that dictate how we must conduct ourselves either as duty or through choice. Naina Devi's was a generation that was trained to respond to the call of duty. Yet, having discharged it under difficult personal circumstances, she was able to go beyond pain, move ahead and follow her own path. Embracing change, she transcended it to create a new life for herself.

Her story begins in Calcutta, still then the glittering first city of the Raj, in the first quarter of the 20th century. The city was the cultural capital of the country, where patrons encouraged music, flocked to the theatre, read the work of distinguished writers led by the likes of Rabindranath Tagore, welcomed the art of the Bengal School and the films of the dazzling young actors, directors and composers who made the Calcutta of those days the centre of the Indian film industry. The young Nilina was the granddaughter of Keshub Chandra Sen, steeped in the liberal afterglow of the Bengal Renaissance and the Brahmo Samaj with their far-reaching social reforms. It was truly said that 'what Bengal thinks today, the rest of the country will think tomorrow'. The city and her home, Lily Cottage, were filled with music, and music became a leitmotif throughout her life. She herself learned to sing under the guidance of the distinguished Girija Shankar Chakravarty and created the opportunities for herself to listen to the leading singers of her time. Her social circle included visits to Jorasanko, the family home of the Tagores, and the Calcutta homes of her aunts—Suniti Devi, Maharani of Cooch Behar and Sucharu Devi, Maharani of Mayurbhanj. Her older sister, Benita Roy, Rani of the Chakma Raj of Rangamati, was a visitor to Lily Cottage.

After her marriage at a young age to Kanwar Ripjit Singh from the Kapurthala royal family, she travelled clear across the country to Simla as Rani Nina Ripjit Singh, the wife of an aristocrat and an eminent landowner of Punjab and what was then the United Provinces, adapting herself to another kind of sophistication and refinement, another culture almost, and certainly another language. Simla was a viceregal city, yet another major city of the British Raj in an era when New Delhi was still finding its feet, an enclave where Indian royal families entertained the viceroys and their splendidly decorated entourages. Her life at that time included idyllic spells in the farmlands of the United Provinces (present-day

Uttar Pradesh) and the charms of its principal city, Lucknow, still basking in an air of Nawabi culture and courtesy, still living its gracious Awadhi lifestyle. During this period she acted as hostess for her father-in-law, when he came to the freshly minted capital city of New Delhi to attend the Council of State where he was appointed as a nominated member.

At this time, in Simla, music was not only not encouraged, it was completely forbidden as an expression for respectable ladies; it was regarded as the art of the *tawaif* (courtesan). Only loose women sang songs other than the sanctioned devotional chanting confined strictly to the privacy of the inner home, the ladies quarters. It was largely a period of silence, the music suppressed, with occasional bursts of expression, which were all the more fervent for being so rare.

Then, after giving birth to four children, she lost her husband at a young age; she was only 32 years old. As her own circumstances changed drastically, she became Naina Devi, seeker of music, who found her peace and her freedom in the world of performance arts. One could argue that her freedom came at a most paradoxical moment when she had to give up her palatial home in Simla and comfortable farmhouse in Rajanagar for a small two-room suite in a modest area of New Delhi, where she and her children had to live. It was in those confines that she began to find herself, where she could be herself; in effect, she was relieved of the burden and limitations of expected behaviours. And she was liberated. She became the singer, Naina Devi.

The stories of Nilina, Nina and Naina Devi appear to belong to totally separate entities. Indeed, they are separated by time, by the ethos of individual phases. How strong that ethos was is one of the points of this book. Yet they remain entwined by character, by personality and by a woman who was very much a person of her times.

NILINA SEN

CALCUTTA: 1917–1935

Nilina and the City of Calcutta

Calcutta in 1917, the year of Nilina Sen's birth, was an exciting place to be. The city shone in the brilliance of an incandescent high noon; it was the capital and the mature first city of the British Empire in India. Some even called it the second city in the whole of the British Empire, next only to London, such was the impact of its mix of British education and disciplines with Indian traditions. Of course, it had already been announced that a new capital city would be constructed in Delhi, but that was still some years away. Meanwhile, the city continued to dazzle, it was metaphorically the last big burst of light for Calcutta as the cultural, administrative and financial centre of the British Raj, which was actually the entire nation because—to all intents and purposes—it also included princely India.

When Nilina was a young girl, before she got married, quite a large part of Calcutta's social structure and outlook directly derived from, or was heavily influenced by, the intensity of its colonial past. A foreign trading company which began its work in India in the 17th century by supplicating the great Mughal Emperors for *farmans* or permission to trade, had—over the years—acquired tremendous power for itself. The path to power was a turbulent one, littered with *farmans* granted and revoked, with peace treaties and negotiations, with practical considerations of business on both sides calling for compromises, with broken promises, violence, the threat of war and war itself. The protagonists were the Mughal Empire, acting through its local authorities, on the one hand and the representatives of the British East India Company on the other.

But neither hostility nor mutual suspicion could stop the inexorable march of events. Buying and selling and trade carried on; the ships sailed out with

View of Fort William, Calcutta, 1735

their cargoes of spices and saltpetre, cotton goods and silks. Towards the end of the 17th century, the Company added legitimacy to its activities by purchasing three villages on the banks of the Hooghly River from local landlords: Sutanuti, Kalikata and Gobindapur. Exactly how significant a step this was, and what it would lead to, could never have been imagined by anybody, not even the merchants of the Company. They had now acquired a legal position within the Mughal Empire with the status of zamindars. They were well and truly established, with a factory for their goods and a willing host of Indian '*banians*' or compradors, go-betweens who were business assistants. At Sutanuti they constructed an early fort for protection against marauders, Fort William, named after King William III of England. Nearby, the embryonic city was taking tentative shape but it would take another fifty-odd years for its outlines to restructure and settle into a south-central European core, the White Town; and the northern area of the Black Town.

Barely five decades later events were precipitated that were about to change the course of history. In 1756, the British enhanced the fortifications of Fort William, a situation viewed with grave mistrust as a threat to his sovereignty by the Nawab of Bengal, Siraj-ud-Daulah. His suspicion was fuelled by the granting of asylum by the British to a man who had embezzled money from the *dewani* of Dhaka. He ordered the British to cease their work on the fort. Angered when they ignored his orders, he attacked and took Calcutta. The chain of subsequent events (including the exaggerated accounts of the infamous Black Hole of Calcutta) led to the Battle of Plassey (or Palashi) in 1757 between the Nawab and Robert Clive, to its twists and treacherous turns, and Siraj-ud-Daulah's defeat and ultimately, his death. The endgame came with the Battle of Buxar seven years later, which pitted the forces of the British East India Company against the combined armies of Nawab Mir Qasim of Bengal; the Nawab of Awadh, Shuja-ud-Daulah; and the Mughal

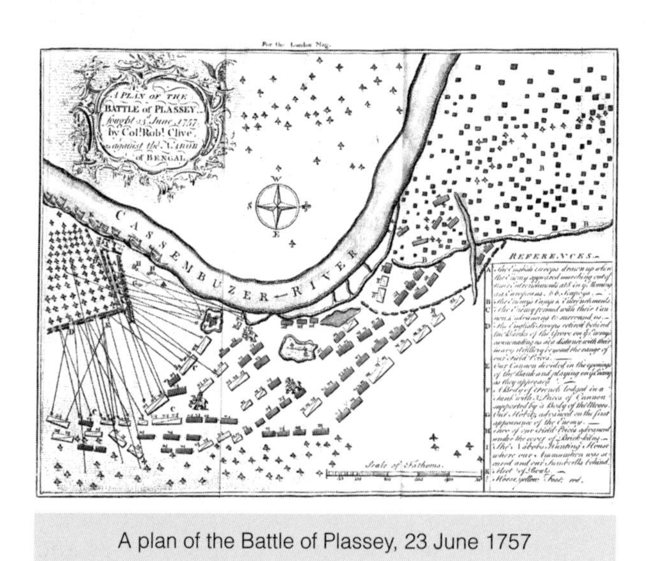

A plan of the Battle of Plassey, 23 June 1757

Emperor, Shah Alam II. However this coalition fell apart, because of internal dissensions and a basic lack of coordination, and the British scored a decisive victory that opened up the rich areas of Bengal and Awadh for them. It was the beginning of the stamp of Empire and of Calcutta as its first city.

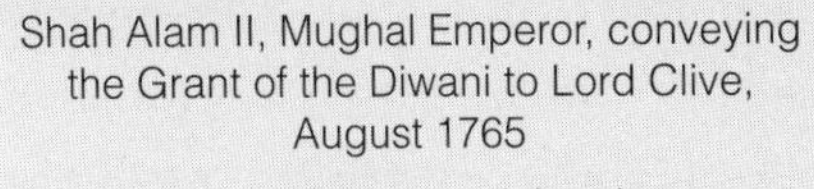

Shah Alam II, Mughal Emperor, conveying the Grant of the Diwani to Lord Clive, August 1765

RIGHT Robert Clive examining the enemy lines from the roof of the Nawab's hunting lodge

Their position secured, the British widened their influence on the growing city of Calcutta. Already in 1752, the East India Company had ordered its functionary, Zepaniah Holwell, to divide the Black Town into separate quarters for different trades. One such quarter, Kalutola, was where Nilina's distinguished ancestor, Ram Kamal Sen, settled; not far away was the quarter of Jorasanko, where the home of the Tagore family was situated. The two families were to have multiple and profound connections that lasted well into the 20th century.

The most influential Indians of those times were the *banians* and *dewans*, the brokers and intermediaries of the British. They functioned as interpreters; kept their accounts and books, negotiated for them, disbursed monies for them; in short, facilitated all those business functions which the British could not carry out themselves, because of lack of language and cultural mismatches. The earliest of the *banians* came from outside Calcutta, merchants drawn to the growing city because it was rapidly becoming a centre of trade in the safe environs of Fort William. They were quite happy

Calcutta, view of sailing ships and other boats docked along the River Hooghly (unknown date)

to acknowledge the suzerainty of the British and offer their services in what were clearly growth areas, and they revelled in the status that this bestowed upon them.

Many of these influential Indians became legends in their own times as they acquired fabulous wealth. Ratan Sarkar was a dhobi or washerman by birth. His destiny guided him to mistakenly answer a call for a *dobhashi* or interpreter, a job he was surely not equipped to undertake. But his own sharpness and ability propelled him forward, and he rose to become one of the richest men in the city.

Perhaps the best known of these newly rich Calcuttans was Nabakrishna Deb, founder of the Sovabazar (Shobha Bazar) Raj, and its Rajbari or palace. He operated from a position of exceptional influence, both as the Persian tutor of Warren Hastings as well as an unofficial intelligence gatherer for Robert Clive, the victor of Plassey. It was he who supplied Clive with vital

Idol of the Goddess Durga during Durga Puja celebrations at Sovabazar, Calcutta

information on the Nawab, Siraj-ud-Daulah, which helped him to overthrow the latter. He was duly rewarded by the British with the title of Raja Bahadur and became the political intermediary between the Indian princes and the East India Company. The floodgates of wealth opened up: eight crores from Siraj-ud-Daulah's treasury are said to have been appropriated by him and two others, a stupendous sum for those times.

Clearly Nabakrishna Deb believed in displaying his wealth and became something of a pioneer in how he chose to do so. He was the first Bengali to drive a coach and pair. He is said to have initiated the custom of a large and public observance of Durga Puja by hosting the very first one in 1757, a huge occasion at which Clive himself was present, ironically to celebrate the British victory at Plassey. In the years that followed, the Puja celebrations elsewhere in Calcutta could only start after his had opened, loudly announced by the firing of cannon. When his mother passed away, no expense was spared for the funeral, which was estimated to cost Rs nine lakhs, a very handsome sum at that time. To cement his position with the British and as a goodwill gesture he donated land for the construction of St John's Church in 1784. Even so, he was able to maintain his status as a devout Hindu, for the land gifted had previously been used for Christian burials and was, therefore, 'polluted' and of no use to orthodox Hindus.

Others too amassed wealth, some part of which came from dubious grey areas including bribery, usury and the skimming of the large amounts of money that routinely changed hands. They were amongst the founders of what was called the 'Babu Culture' and their luxurious and lavish lifestyles were the subject of envy and awe. Their aspirations drew from the ripeness of the cultures they much admired: those of the nawabi and landed zamindari aristocracy who lived lives of great luxury with a studied nonchalance for money. Stories of their extravagances unfolded before an astounded and admiring public. One gentleman's entire palace was washed down with costly rose water every single day, nor would he wear a dhoti more than once, petulantly ripping off the expensive borders woven in Dhaka because they scratched his skin. The only utensils he used were made of gold and silver. This kind of conspicuous consumption extended to all manner of lavish celebrations of weddings, family occasions and festivals like Holi and Durga Puja. Sometimes the display of wealth descended into an exercise in vulgarity, for example when cigarettes were lit with ten rupee notes, or the ladies of the night in the red light area of Sonargachhi were gifted with expensive Benarasi saris on the last day of Saraswati Puja.

But the one factor all the wealthy men had in common was the manner in which they entertained their British masters in their palatial homes, the great houses of Calcutta. One historian comments wryly 'to entertain lavishly their British patrons (was) perhaps one of the earliest public relations campaign of the modern era.' All through the second half of the 18th century then sporadically till the middle of the 19th, there were sumptuous dinners and banquets where the host's prestige was much enhanced by the mere presence of the British, and his status rose commensurate with the seniority of his guests. The birthdays of sahibs and mems were also celebrated; when one young lady consented to grace such an occasion her Indian host '...thanked her in very polite terms for having illuminated his house with her bright appearance.' Very often such occasions included a nautch performance, a song and dance performance that imitated the nawabi style, with court dancers and musicians from Murshidabad and Awadh.

These glittering parties were held against the backdrop of the great houses of the Black Town. Such houses were designed to incorporate all the features required for a gracious way of life: open courtyards, some with Italian-style fountains or embellished with statues; the *Thakur Dhalan* or place of worship; the *Nat Mandir* or temple of dramatics, the *Baithak Khana* which was the formal reception room, and the *Jalsaghar*, the hall for music and dance where the nautch performances were held. The public spaces opened out one into the other; discreetly, on the upper floors and towards the back lay the suites of the zenana, the women's wing, hidden behind ornamental grills; and service areas such as the servants' quarters, the strong rooms, offices, stables and granary. Liveried retainers and gate-keepers served those on the premises. A great house was like a self-contained unit, with its marble floors covered with carpets. Light streamed in through coloured glass windows to illuminate, perhaps, ornately framed oil portraits of revered family members or add glitter to grand chandeliers.

But it was the founders of the great houses who initially sparked off the so-called 'Babu Culture', which is seen as a result of the interaction between them and the West. Though the word 'Babu' was originally an honorofic, when it was used in this context it was not necessarily a kind term and reflected the disdain felt by British and Indian alike. The former used it as a derogatory phrase for the Indians they looked down upon as lowly, graceless and unrefined imitators of their own culture; the latter used it mercilessly in countless Bengali satires and farces to lampoon a witless aspiration to a society to which they could never belong. Yet, two generations later, it was the descendants of these very people who contributed personally and financially to the great social and educational reform movements of the 19th century, which we now know as the Bengal Renaissance. They became the generous patrons of the arts, founders of newspapers and journals, enthusiastic supporters of significant institutions like Hindu College, the Calcutta School Book Society, the Calcutta Public Library and the Bengal Social Science Association. They were the drivers of the great movements; without them the requisite next levels of awareness and forward impetus would not have been possible.

Ram Kamal Sen and the Bengal Renaissance

As time progressed from the 18th century to the 19th century, not all Calcutta houses that were large in size were necessarily the great houses of the merchants. Nilina's aunt, Suniti Devi, who was later to become the Maharani of Cooch Behar, remembered her childhood home in Kalutola with great fondness in her autobiography. She wrote:

> Looking back on those days of childhood I have vivid memories of their happiness. The great house seemed an enchanted palace. It is difficult to convey…a real idea of the fascination of its cool, silent interior with the six courtyards, and the deep wells which supplied drinking and bathing water. In the zenana part of the establishment where the strict purdah ladies lived, the rooms ran round one of these courtyards, and the ladies were never allowed to walk outside it. When they went into town, the 'palkis' came right inside to fetch them. I remember wonderful games of hide-and-seek which we children played about the courtyards and the old house.
>
> The whole of the domestic arrangements at Coolootola (Kalutola) were on patriarchal lines, and strange to relate, family quarrels were rare, although there was a very large number of women living together under the same roof. When I say that our household included fifty relations, some idea of the size of the establishment will be arrived at.

Keshub Chandra Sen, prominent leader of the Brahmo Samaj and social reformer

Suniti Devi lived during an era when far-reaching social changes had begun to take place and would continue to take place throughout her lifetime. She was the daughter of Keshub Chandra Sen, the grandfather of Nilina Sen. He was a committed social reformer, leading light of the Brahmo Samaj and renowned figure of the Bengal Renaissance. Such was the lustre of his life and achievement that we tend to overlook *his* remarkable grandfather, Ram Kamal Sen, who in so many ways set the stage for Keshub Chandra's accomplishments and indeed those of his descendants. If there was ever a story of a spectacular rise wrenched out of sheer grit and application, it was that of Ram Kamal.

He was born in a village on the banks of the Hooghly River called Gariffa. He was still only a little boy when he left the village for Calcutta, determined to get an education. Indeed, this determination was a hallmark of his life and it enabled him to progress far beyond the daunting circumstances of his early career. He had learnt English, Sanskrit and Persian and was only 17 years old when he began working as a clerk's assistant; his next job was with the Hindoostanee Press as a compositor for eight rupees a month. The salary was rather meagre, no doubt, but he worked hard and displayed great capabilities; and this caught the attention of the eminent Orientalist and Secretary of the Asiatic Society, Horace H. Wilson, who was quick to spot the youngster's potential and made him a protégé.

There was no looking back after that. He rose to become the Native Manager of the Hindoostanee Press, then the Native Secretary of the Asiatic Society

Keshub Chandra Sen's close-knit family: 'a circle of love and care'

for whose journal he wrote several articles. His rise encompassed many and varied activities over the years: among other things, he became the Treasurer of the Bank of Bengal with the title of Dewan and helped to set up institutions such as the Calcutta Medical College and the Indian Museum. One of his major contributions was the compilation of a comprehensive two-volume English-Bengali dictionary explaining some 58,000 words. In the second volume, the introduction incorporated a linguistic analysis of the Bengali language as well as a history of Bengali prose from 1800. This was widely acknowledged as a meticulous and comprehensive work, a valuable addition to the scholarship of the time.

His great interest in matters of education was very apparent and he was associated with the Hindu College and the newly-established Sanskrit College. Certainly this is an interest that he passed on to his grandson, upon whom he doted, who in turn believed passionately in the value of education and made it the driver for many of his activities. And it was inherited by Keshub Chandra Sen's daughters, who occupied pre-eminent positions in society as the Maharanis of Cooch Behar and Mayurbhanj, and for whom the education of women became a central cause in their own lives.

Sir William Jones, portrait in the Hall of University College, Oxford

Yet Ram Kamal Sen himself remained a person of great simplicity. Without doubt he was a man of great distinction in the city of Calcutta, a polymath, who was not only intellectually gifted in a variety of fields, but also a brilliant organizer and administrator. By the time he passed away in the mid-19th century his earnings enabled him to leave wealth and a sizable estate for his heirs, including the large house in Kalutola. But his biography describes a preference for a life of personal frugality, a man who repudiated the flamboyance of his time for modest clothing and one simple meal a day.

Ram Kamal Sen's youthful and lasting association with the Asiatic Society opened many doors for him and distinguished him as one of the early participants in the giant social, intellectual and cultural movement that we now know as the Bengal Renaissance. The Asiatic Society, founded in 1784, was like a scholarly club for the Orientalists who clustered around its ambit. Its founder, Sir William Jones, began with a dream; his vision was that of a centre for Asian studies which included history, scriptures, geography, mathematics and mixed sciences, music, agriculture and commerce, among many other things. And such was his enthusiasm that the Society was actually founded within four months of his arrival in India. The studies he dreamt of became the principal thrust of the Asiatic Society and they were steeped in the spirit of scientific enquiry which was the legacy of 18th century Enlightenment.

The studies William Jones pursued included comparative linguistics between Greek, Latin and Sanskrit, and the results suggested a common heritage between the three, leading to the concept of an Indo-European family of languages. Such studies posed challenges to the entrenched concepts of the Western scholars of that time, whose view of human civilization was very Eurocentric, not to mention arrogant. It was a significant attitudinal shift and it was voiced by Jones himself who called Asia the 'nurse of sciences' and the 'inventress of delightful and useful arts'. In a letter to Warren Hastings, he admitted, 'We are like savages who thought that the sun set and rose for them alone'.

Despite this, and the close interaction between traditional Indian knowledge holders like the pandits and Western scholars, the social equations between the Indians and the British were anything but equal. The strange titles given to Ram Kamal Sen of 'Native' manager and 'Native' secretary have a pejorative ring, an implication of lower standards which are purely based on race. The glittering nautch parties of the late 18th century hosted by the wealthy Indians of the Black Town had now become few and far between, and more-or-less tapered off completely after the middle of the 19th century. There was a hardening of polarities, and after the War of Independence of

1857 the divide between the colonized and their colonial masters became a virtual wall.

Some historians see the researches and work of the Asiatic Society and the Orientalist movement as the backdrop for the expressions of the Bengal Renaissance. Certainly the vast scope of those studies brought out the sweep and grandeur of ancient Indian civilization and was a source of pride to the educated Indians of Calcutta, and perhaps restored to them some sense of cultural identity. For too long they had been battered by the criticism and scorn heaped on Indian traditions and beliefs by proselytising Christian missionaries and the colonial regime. Yet less than six decades later, the Orientalists were being cast aside, their efforts derided by the likes of Macaulay, who rejected Oriental learning and supported instead only English education for Indians, believing that this would erase superstition and medieval thinking from India. Macaulay's goal was to create '... a class of persons, Indian in blood and colour but English in taste, in opinions, in morals and in intellect...'

The belief in the benefits of Western education was shared by a number of Indians. The year 1817 saw the founding of Hindu College (its name belied its secular curriculum), the first English language college in India which was focused on the study of Western thought, through its philosophers and great literary figures. Here Indian youths learnt to develop critical thinking and individualism. It later became the Presidency College and was one of the premier institutions associated with the Bengal Renaissance.

The term 'Bengal Renaissance' has been variously interpreted and hotly contested by historians, but the fact remains that it was a very distinct movement in 19th century Bengal, a sort of intellectual awakening which saw the flowering of remarkable talents in a variety of fields: in social and religious reform, in education and literature, in pure sciences and art, in journalism and oratory, to name just a few. As a movement it brought many great figures to national attention, such as the brilliant social reformer Raja Ram Mohan Roy, founder of the religious reform movement the Brahmo Samaj (originally named the Brahmo Sabha) in 1828, who campaigned

Raja Ram Mohan Roy, statue at College Green, Bristol

TOP MIDDLE Ishwar Chandra Vidyasagar, (photograph taken before 1891)

TOP RIGHT Bankim Chandra Chatterjee from *The Literature of Bengal*, 1895

EXTREME RIGHT Rabindranath Tagore, before 1941

RIGHT Sarat Chandra Chatterjee

vigorously against suttee; the writer and publisher Ishwarchandra Vidyasagar, who fought for widow remarriage and against child marriage; Keshub Chandra Sen, a leader of the Brahmo Samaj, who was known as the Martin Luther of India; writers such as Bankim Chandra Chatterjee and Sarat Chandra Chatterjee who would be decisive shapers of Bengali literature; and of course the Tagore family, culminating in the genius of Rabindranath Tagore, whose contributions could well constitute a total renaissance by themselves.

You might call this a 'rebirth' or 're-awakening' caused by the combination of two streams, the traditions of the Indian cultural past mingled with the disciplines of Western intellectual and scientific thought which brought modernization and revitalization in its wake. From the beginning, it was

a movement that addressed a distinctly elitist urban audience; and in the main, it was this very section that responded to the movement. It is an irony of history that this ferment, this churning, this renewed creativity, which was so directly a result of Western thinking, came at a time when relations between the two races were very poor.

Not all reformers agreed all the time about which changes called for priority. From within the progressive Sen family, Ram Kamal Sen was a staunch opponent of Ram Mohan Roy since he himself was an orthodox person who believed in suttee. Keshub Chandra Sen thought that education for women should equip them only to be better housewives and family members but frowned on more radical ideas as he felt that change, to be acceptable, should be gradual. But of his impact on the Brahmo Samaj and the support he generated as its most ardent proponent there can be no doubt.

Keshub Chandra Sen: 'One God, One Life, One Wife'

In contemporary times, it seems as if the entire belief system that we know as the Brahmo Samaj has vanished into the mists of the past, forgotten by all except perhaps a handful of followers and a few historians. Difficult, then, for us to imagine exactly how radical this reform was two centuries ago when it was first introduced to an amazed section of upper-class Bengali Brahmin Hindus. It was an altogether pioneering effort: the first religious reform to emerge from within the Hindu tradition, a reform that also covered other social issues concerning women, their education and their status. Like all reform movements, it went through its ups and downs, its disagreements and reconciliations, its splits and schisms. The Brahmo Samaj (or Brahmo Sabha, as it was then known) was founded by Raja Ram Mohan Roy in 1828, and over the next 50 years transmuted into the Brahmo Samaj; it appeared and reappeared in various new forms, such as the Adi Brahmo Samaj, the Brahmo Samaj of India, the Naba Bidhan or New Dispensation and the Sadharan Brahmo Samaj. Broadly speaking, all of them followed the basic constructs of Brahmoism, based on the concept of a universalist theistic society. The reason for these manifold existences was either a spirited response to what was considered 'old' thinking, or an immediate reaction to an unpopular decision or a nuanced change in perception. Again, like all major movements, it threw up personalities who were great thinkers and social activists, visionary men with a gift for articulation, communicating with audiences who were ripe to receive the progressive messages they put forth.

Debendranath Tagore, father of Rabindranath Tagore, by Abanindranath Tagore

Prominent among these was Nilina's grandfather, Keshub Chandra Sen, one of the most charismatic figures of the Brahmo Samaj, indeed, one might say, of the entire movement of the Bengal Renaissance. He had a magnetic personality, and exuded the full force of his conviction through brilliant oratory which combined 'wonderful mastery of the English language... extraordinary wealth of imagination...soul-compelling moral idealism'. Add to this a sonorous voice, clear diction and enormous presence and one can understand how he was able to bring about the conversion of a large number of Bengali youth to the Brahmo faith; as one admirer wrote, '...when he spoke, the world listened...'

Indeed, his mentor Debendranath Tagore (the father of Rabindranath Tagore) noticed his oratorical skills at their very first meeting. At that time, Debendranath, then a leading light of the Brahmo Samaj, was himself quite a figure at the age of 40, 'a tall princely man in the full glory of his health and his manhood...' Keshub was a mature 20-year old, already steeped in his spiritual quest and addressing a rapt audience at the Goodwill Fraternity Club when he was first sighted. The bonding was instant. Debendranath saw in him 'a saintly youth', 'to me dearer than my son'. Keshub,

Dwarkanath Tagore, bust at the National Library, Kolkata

who had lost his father when only a young boy, recognized in Debendranath both an inspiration for his quest and a missing father figure.

Debendranath had inherited the faith from his own father, 'Prince' Dwarkanath Tagore, one of the original signatories to the trust deed signed in 1830 for the property of the Prayer Hall, the first place of worship of the Adi Brahmo Samaj, which also laid out the tenets of the faith. Prior to that, the early assemblies were basically informal meetings of family and friends convened by Raja Ram Mohan Roy. The trust deed set forth 'the worship and adoration of the Eternal Unsearchable and Immutable Being who is the Author and Preserver of the Universe, but not under or by any other name designation or title…', cutting out the multiple deities of the Hindu faith in favour of the One Deity, Brahman, the Supreme Being, who was formless. There would be no images and idols for worship, no sacrifice of animals, no 'feasting or rioting'. This was an echo of widely-held contemporary Christian thought that Indians were largely 'idolaters, blindly attached to doctrines and rites' and inclined towards superstition. Significantly, the trust deed forbade adherents to revile or speak contemptuously of anything that was an object of worship for 'any man or set of men'. At the same time, it laid down that that 'no sermon, preaching, discourse, prayer or hymn be delivered, made or used in such worship but such as have a tendency to the promotion of the contemplation of the Author and Preserver of the Universe, to the promotion of charity, morality, piety, benevolence, virtue and the strengthening the bonds of union between men of all religious persuasions and creeds'.

Such was the manner in which that early trust deed laid out the provisions under which the new faith would eventually operate as a monotheistic reformist movement. It carried all the hallmarks of the great sweeping movements of the time: a reimagining of a rooted Indian tradition cast in a very Western and Christian mould. Thus, the references to an Immutable, almost abstract, Being, moving away from the innumerable beloved gods of Hinduism; thus the prohibition of image worship foreshadowing Macaulay's stated goal of removing idolatry from young Indian minds. Quite obviously this was not a religion for the common man. At the same time, at the very heart and foundation of the early Brahmo Samaj lay the ancient texts of the Vedanta, therefore clearly there was no intention of alienating an entire Hindu body.

Yet alienate it did. Those who subscribed to the new faith were cast out of the old. When Keshub Chandra Sen decided to join the Brahmo Samaj, it meant cutting ties with his family and leaving his own home to seek shelter in the home of Debendranath Tagore. It created a marked, though temporary, rift in the family, of which his daughter Suniti Devi gives a poignant and romantic description in her autobiography:

> He must have gone through much trouble of mind before he decided to fly in the face of family tradition and take a step which meant partial separation from his nearest and dearest. My mother was a member of a strict Hindu family, and their marriage had been solemnised with Hindu rites; but she did not fail him in the hour of trial...When he announced his approaching conversion, the 'Sen House' was plunged into a state of agitation, and my mother was by turns entreated and threatened by angry and dismayed relatives.
>
> 'Do not go against our customs', urged the purdah ladies...'You must not renounce your caste. Imagine the results of such a dreadful sin.' When thus reproached, the young girl dreaded the horrors of the unknown. It may be that she wavered; but if so, it was not for long; and it was arranged that she should go with my father to be converted by the Maharshi D. Tagore. On the day fixed for their departure, a note came. My father had written simply, 'I am waiting.' Then my mother knew she must decide her future for good and all. All the relations were screaming, crying, and threatening my mother, saying that she would bring disgrace on the family by leaving the house, and thus losing her caste. But it did not hinder her, because of those three simple words 'I am waiting' the call of Love. When she realised their meaning, she threw off the fetters of the past and went forth to meet her destiny... Fearfully she descended the dark steps, her heart beating with fright, until at last she saw my father. He said quietly: 'I want you to realise your position fully. If you come with me, you give up caste, rank, money, and jewels. The relations who love you will become estranged

> from you. The bread of bitterness will be your portion. You will lose all except me. Am I worth the sacrifice?'
>
> ...They looked into each other's eyes. He read perfect faith and courage in hers. She saw in his a love which gave her confidence to face the future. They passed down the corridor and found themselves in the first courtyard opposite the great entrance, where the durwans (gatekeepers) were standing on guard.
>
> ...My father, seeing that the durwans would not open the door, went to lift the bar and did so quite easily. Then a voice was heard speaking from the upper floor. It was my father's eldest brother. He had watched all that had happened, and, seeing that my parents were determined, he decided to let them go.
>
> 'Let them pass, and open the gate,' he called out to the durwans. The wondering durwans threw open the door, and my parents passed from the shadows into the sunlight.
>
> My father took my mother to the beautiful house of Maharshi Debendranath Tagore. The house-hold were all waiting to welcome them, though they had great doubts whether my father would be able to bring my mother away from such a strict Hindu family. The Maharshi introduced my mother to his daughters as if she had been his own child.
>
> ...My parents remained away for some time during which my father's formal conversion took place. After some months my grandmother and uncle begged him to return, and gave him a small house near the big house. There my parents lived until my father fell seriously ill, and his eldest brother declared that, in spite of all difficulties, he must come back to the old home. He came back, and after long suffering and much careful nursing grew well again.

Some of this suffering might well have been a depletion of nervous energy. Romain Rolland described Sen as 'a being exhausting itself in searching after God.' People accused him of inconsistency, following now one credo and now another, swaying from a semi-Christian austerity to effusions of Hindu mysticism; however, he was certainly consistent in one area: he never abandoned his spiritual search, whatever the path, whatever the destination.

There was a time when he was so inclined towards Christianity, speaking of Christ as 'the brightest jewel of my heart, the necklace of my soul', that even Debendranath felt he might convert. Then came a return to his Vaishnav roots; and there is a description of him singing kirtans with tears running down his face, using the devotional singing, dancing and street processions, *sankirtana* and *nagarakirtana*, of the Chaitanya movement as expressions of faith. At one point his most obsessive thought was the reconciliation of man with man, in pursuit of which he brought together, for the first time, excerpts from the great scriptures of Hinduism, Christianity, Islam, and other faiths in his *Shlokasangraha*, the book of devotional lessons. Inscribed on its title page was 'The Wide Universe is the Temple of God'. This universalism was reflected in the architecture of the mandir of the Brahmo Samaj of India in 1869 which was a blend of church, temple and mosque, 'paying reverence to all truths that exist in the world.' It was the expression of a strong belief in the basic one-ness of the human heart yearning for the Divine amidst the diversity of this world.

But by then he had long parted ways with Debendranath Tagore. There were surface issues of casteism and the use of the sacred thread, symbols of the pangs of growing pains where the older man felt that change and the reformation of Hindu identity should be a gradual process whereas a younger faction believed that it should be precipitated rapidly and more democratically. Thus, after the inevitable schism, by 1866 Debendranath Tagore headed the Adi (or Original) Brahmo Samaj and Keshub Chandra Sen the newly-created Brahmo Samaj of India.

In 1870, Sen went to England. He was already widely perceived as an Anglophile loyal to British rule. Here he met Queen Victoria at Osbourne House on the Isle of Wight and gifted her with a portrait of his wife. In return he received inscribed copies of her books. In an atmosphere where nationalism was on the rise he was severely criticized for his audience with Queen Victoria and for declaring, 'We love our Queen as our mother'. And yet, in one of those apparent *volte faces* he was known for, he thundered during a lecture on England's Duties to India, 'If England seeks to crush down two hundred

millions of people in this glorious country, to destroy their nationality, to extinguish the fire of noble antiquity...and if England's object of governing the people of India is to simply make money, then I say perish the British Rule this moment!' We may imagine what a sensation this caused and the vituperation it evoked from the Anglo-Indian press. But he simply stated, 'I came here an Indian, I go back a confirmed Indian.'

Clearly the 'confirmed Indian' had absorbed much on this trip to England. On his return, he threw himself into significant social activism by establishing the Indian Reform Association. A major shift in thinking was the realization that if society was really to improve, the change had to address and include peasants and workers, the underprivileged who, at this time, simply did not exist in the perceptions of the Bengali middle class. It is claimed, though on what basis is not known, that this was the influence of Karl Marx whom Keshub Chandra is alleged to have met on this trip to Europe. This is not clearly documented, nor has it been proved, but the fact remains that the concepts of mass education and cheap access to information and news were introduced here, both for the first time. Industrial arts schools were set up to teach skills such as tailoring, clock repair, printing and lithography. The earliest journalistic effort aimed at uplifting and bringing news to the masses came with a paper that cost just one pice, *Sulabh Samachar*, which quickly became very popular because it not only gave its readers information in simple and easy to read Bengali, but also served as a voice for the poor, raising matters that concerned them. Above all, it was cheap and easily available.

But in this very decade of the 1870s, Keshub Chandra Sen was to face perhaps his most major challenge, a falling-out so extreme that it split the Brahmo Samaj yet again, causing him to form the Naba Bidhan or New Dispensation. This time, the schism emerged from a very personal issue, that of the marriage of his daughter, Suniti Devi to Maharaja Nripendra Narayan Bhup Bahadur of Cooch Behar.

There were several contexts to this, one of them being the Brahmo Marriage Act of 1872, a source of acrimonious contention amongst the different

Lily Cottage, the Sen home where Nilina was born

factions of the faith, but passed under heavy pressure and unsparing effort from Keshub Chandra. The Act was necessitated by the fact that Brahmo marriages had been officially ruled as invalid and the children born of these illegitimate since they did not conform to Hindu rites; it also laid down the minimum age for bride and groom at fourteen years and eighteen years respectively. Much publicity was given to the fact that these ages had been scientifically decided in consultation with doctors.

Another context was his purchase, in October 1877, of a property with extensive grounds and a pool, called Lily Cottage. When it got known that the marriage of Suniti Devi, aged 13, had been arranged with the young Maharaja of Cooch Behar, a tidal wave of protest and abuse engulfed him. He was accused of many things: being a hypocrite since his daughter was below the minimum age; having 'sold' his daughter to the 'jungly' Maharaja of Cooch Behar for monetary considerations; having bought Lily Cottage (with Brahmo funds) for the sole purpose of impressing the royal family of Cooch Behar; of living a lavish lifestyle and betraying the very reformist

ideals that he had propagated. Afterwards, outraged members of the Brahmo Samaj of India claimed that marriage was conducted according to Hindu and not Brahmo rites; in short, the entire matter became a scandal of epic proportions.

Wearily, Sen wrote to a friend:

> My antagonists have impeached my character, showered upon me abusive epithets of all kinds, and represented me before the public as one who, for fame and wealth and worldly advantages, has unhesitatingly sold his conscience and his daughter! This is indeed the substance of the charges preferred against me, and an insinuation to this effect is to be found, I am told, in the so-called protest. If my conscience acquits me, none can convict me. Of this I am sure, that I never sought a Rajah. I never coveted filthy lucre...I was acting all along as a public man...The British Government sought me and my daughter; a Christian Government that knew me thoroughly to be a Brahmo leader, proposed the alliance, and the weighty interests of a State were pressed upon me with a view to induce me to accept the proposal and make the needful concessions.

The irony is that Keshub Chandra Sen, so vilified, was not making excuses but simply telling the truth; unfortunately there was much that did not become evident until long after his death. The sequence was quite logical in its unfolding and clear to follow. The alliance was arranged by the British Government who had supervised the upbringing of the young fatherless Maharaja; now that he was about to set sail for England to pursue his studies it was imperative that he marry an educated Indian girl—the British were only too aware of awkward and thoroughly unsuitable alliances encountered overseas and their unhappy consequences. The Maharaja's family had to be assured that only an Indian girl would be the future Maharani before they would accept his going to England; but in the best interests of a state that was regarded as backward and tribal, where practices like polygamy prevailed, it was necessary for the future bride to come from a civilized milieu, such that she could be a suitable companion to carry out the reforms the British saw as essential.

The ceremony of 1878 was a marriage, true enough, and in the presence of Hindu priests. But it remained unconsummated, and Suniti came back to Lily Cottage where she stayed with her parents until she was 16 years old. By this time, the Maharaja had already returned from England and had joined Presidency College in Calcutta; he had, to all intents and purposes, become a member of the Brahmo faith and attended the religious service regularly every Sunday. In her autobiography Suniti Devi describes her 'real' marriage which took place in the Temple of the New Dispensation, after which she went to live with her husband.

With this marriage Keshub Chandra Sen had effectively acted as missionary in a new space. He had transmitted his zeal for social reform, upliftment and education to both daughter and son-in-law. Within 15 years of assuming the *gaddi* in 1883, the Maharaja had embarked upon a series of programmes: the improvement of communications through the building of roads, bridges and a railway line; establishing health care with hospitals and dispensaries; founding a girls school, a college; offering his people public parks and gardens, to name only some. Significantly, he announced that the state religion would be the Brahmoism of the New Dispensation and built a huge church or temple, the largest in the country, to give physical embodiment to that decision.

Ramakrishna in a trance (state of *samadhi*) supported by his nephew Hriday and surrounded by Brahmo devotees. At the house of Keshub Chandra Sen, Calcutta, 21 September 1879

In the last decade of his life, yet another figure appeared in Keshub Chandra Sen's life: this was a meeting that added a new curve to his oft re-moulded ideology. And its reverberations echoed around the world in ways he could not have foreseen. Around 1875 he met the Hindu mystic, Shri Ramakrishna, and surely no two religious

personalities could have been more unlike in being and in beliefs. And yet, as a historian has recorded, 'The attraction was mutual; the influence was mutual.' It must have been helped by Shri Ramakrishna's own unassuming nature, his even-handed reverence for all religions, his ability to voice profound truths in simple words and his soothing acceptance that God could be formless as much as He could take on a form—important in a faith that banned idolatry. From that point onwards, the two met and Keshub Chandra was swayed by the mystic's concept of the Motherhood of God, which he incorporated into his own thinking. 'If God is father-like, He is surely mother-like too,' he wrote. And again, in his autobiography, 'Now that I have seen Mother I feel as if I would be forever maddened by joy...'

Swami Vivekananda, Chicago, September, 1893. On the left, in his own handwriting, 'one infinite pure and holy—beyond thought beyond qualities I bow down to thee'.

Among his young associates in the New Dispensation at that time was Narendranath Datta, who participated in Brahmo activities and loved to sing Brahmo songs. He acted the role of Yogi in Keshub Chandra's play, 'Naba Brindaban' and it was clear that he was marked out for leadership. He was introduced to Shri Ramakrishna by Keshub Chandra. That crucial meeting led to Narendranath eventually leaving Brahmoism and becoming a disciple of Shri Ramakrishna where he adopted the name of Vivekananda. And the rest, as they say, is history.

A cenotaph on the grounds of Lily Cottage

Keshub Chandra Sen passed away in 1884 at the age of 46, a young demise following a life of extraordinary richness, yet fraught with challenges on many fronts and riven with strife. In early January of that year, ill and exhausted, and against the advice of his doctors, he was carried to a new sanctuary in the grounds of Lily Cottage to consecrate it. Here he offered his last prayers and passed away a few days later, much to the sorrow and despair of his followers. Two years before his death, as he lay stricken with diabetes, he had said to one of his disciples, 'To me the state of being on fire is the state of salvation...From when I was young I have always kept burning the fire of enthusiasm...'

Could there be an obituary more brief yet so telling?

The Sen family

Even this short account of the spiritual journey of Keshub Chandra Sen shows what a very active man he must have been. He travelled to spread the faith, enthralling his audiences with poetic visions of the syncretic God, he travelled to gather support for his social reforms which inspired the hope of new possibilities for the less privileged and he even went to England, which he called 'my Father's Western house' to study the Christian life.

Yet he managed to make time for his children, and Suniti Devi's autobiography gives us insights into that family life and the personalities who were part of it. Until the purchase of Lily Cottage, her childhood was spent in a house on the grounds of Kalutola, that large joint family home, though many gatherings in the main house were forbidden to them because they were Brahmos and no longer Hindus. As she grew up she felt like an outsider during festivities because of this loss of caste. Only from a distance could she inhale the fragrance of incense or tune her ears to the faint sounds of conch shells and bells when her grandmother offered evening prayers in front of the idol.

But then there were the innumerable Sen children to play with. Afternoons on the roof were a special time which she remembered with fond nostalgia: 'I loved that hour, and the memory of it often comes back to me. I close my eyes and dream I am a child again sitting in the midst of that happy group...'

The head of the household was Suniti's handsome grandmother, a formidable lady who 'exacted and received the utmost deference from her daughters-in-law.' Quite obviously they neither raised their eyes nor spoke to their husbands in her presence. But somewhere under that tough exterior lay a soft spot for Suniti who, unlike the others, was never afraid of her. The fact that the grandmother herself did a lot of the housework and much of the cooking—unusual for a family of such wealth—was, perhaps, a reflection of the grounded values of their ancestor Ram Kamal Sen.

If there was exclusion in certain areas for Keshub Chandra's children, elsewhere there was open-armed inclusion. The ten children—five girls and five boys—realized very early in their lives that their father was a special person, a public figure whose charisma and personality attracted followers. It helped that he had a commanding physical presence, tall and broad shouldered, that his voice was so clear that it could be heard across crowds of people, that what he had to say was so appealing to so many. It also helped that he included his family in his mission in the most profound ways. Sometimes the older children would set off from Kalutola to accompany him on his religious excursions (as Suniti Devi described such travels) by train or in a box-like horse carriage. They loved the religious services conducted by their father: clearly those young experiences left a deep impress on Suniti Devi. In her autobiography, she wrote:

> I have another vivid memory of those days: sometimes, long before the servants were awake, a beautiful voice filled the dawn with melody. It was one of my father's missionaries who, alone upon the roof, sang the praise of God in that sweet and silent hour. I can hear the echo of his song even now. We children used to think that we were very near to heaven then…

There was even an experiment in congregational living; two houses built near Kalutola accommodated many of Keshub Chandra Sen's followers and their families, as a community. Here they worked together and prayed together as one big united family, addressing each other as sisters and aunts, uncles and brothers. And here Keshub Chandra held a service each morning, his motto being 'Faith, Love and Purity'.

But above all there was the warm embrace of their own family, there was their gentle pretty mother with her tiny hands and feet and her wealth of dark hair who sang them songs in Bengali and put them to sleep by telling them fairy tales. Gentle and petite she might have been, but she held strong convictions and was a courageous support for her husband; she faced her loss of caste in the Hindu world without expressing distress or resentment; the world, as her daughter wrote, never troubled her. And then there were the siblings, the five sons and five daughters forming their own circle of love and care.

Suniti Devi was the oldest daughter and deeply attached to her siblings, especially the older among them, with whom she had grown up. She became, as we have seen, the Maharani of Cooch Behar, but she was not the only one of Keshub Chandra Sen's daughters to marry into a royal family. Her sister, Savitri, married the Maharaja's cousin and joined her in Cooch Behar. She was of great help to Suniti and assisted her with the many projects that were always being undertaken in the fields of education and public health.

Another active collaborator in social reform was the third sister, Sucharu, who became the Maharani of Mayurbhanj, a princely state of some size, which was one of the three states of the Bengal States Agency in the Raj era. Her marriage took place in 1904 when she was 30 years old and well beyond what would have been regarded as a suitable age for a lady of that time. In many ways the story of her marriage was diametrically the opposite of that of Suniti Devi. She was engaged while still a girl to the Maharaja of Mayurbhanj, Shri Sriram Chandra Bhanj Deo (under what circumstances is not recorded), but his family did not approve as she was not only a Brahmo but the daughter of a very prominent leader of the faith. A marriage with a devout and traditional Hindu ruler was quite out of the question (and in this case there was no pressure from the British as the ruler himself was well inclined toward reform), and the Maharaja eventually married a princess from Chhotanagpur.

That must have been a quite a blow for Sucharu Devi, but she remained loyal to the Maharaja. In her autobiography Suniti Devi wrote,

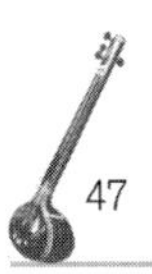

Keshub Chandra Sen's third daughter, Sucharu Devi, Maharani of Mayurbhanj, seen with her children in this elegant portrait

> We tried to persuade her to marry, but nothing would induce her to forget…Fourteen years passed, during which she was an angel in our house. Then she found her long-delayed happiness. The Maharajah's wife died, and he came back to ask my sister to marry him. The marriage took place in Calcutta, and for some time the Maharajah and my sister led the happiest of lives…

But in Calcutta they remained. It is a matter of record that the opposition to their marriage from his family had not abated, and as a consequence during the Maharaja's lifetime she was never taken to the Mayurbhanj Palace in the capital city of Baripada, a majestic building with Corinthian columns and vast wooden doors engraved with royal insignias. They had to live apart for long intervals, a cause of anxiety and distress. Sujata, the youngest of the Sen sisters, narrated in a biography of Sucharu Devi that once she had actually packed her bags and begged her husband to take her with him, but he had refused. Quite possibly, he saw his own family's opposition as an obstacle which could only be worn down with the passage of time. Instead he built her Rajabagh, a beautiful residence in Calcutta set in the midst of extensive gardens. Here, as Sucharu Devi's biographer records, 'many distinguished visitors were entertained; there were Viceroys, Governors, Ministers and men and women from the creative world of art and writing, for the Maharaja enjoyed entertaining and being lavish in his hospitality.' Perhaps this is not the life that she anticipated, but it was a reality that she had to accept.

Sadly, she was not fated to enjoy a long marriage with a husband for whom she had waited for so many years. The Maharaja was in a hunting party for bears near Baripada one winter evening as twilight was setting in. He descended from the machan and, in his long black coat, was mistaken for a bear by a member of the party and accidentally shot, dying of septicemia a few days later. Sucharu Devi lived on for almost half a century, during which time she had to cope with another terrible loss, that of her son who died in action as an RAF pilot during World War II.

But she was very much her father's daughter; although she was very young when he died, his influence was discernable in many of her activities, especially her deep interest in the education of women. The Maharani Girls High School in Darjeeling is a testament to this: founded in 1908 by Hemlata Sarkar, it was funded by both Maharani Suniti Devi as well as Maharani Sucharu Devi, hence its name. She was responsible for setting up the Women's Educational Board and was associated with many institutions, including the Victoria Institute that her father had established. She remained active in social causes through her life, as a Life Member of the Indian Red Cross Society, as the President of the All Bengal Women's Union, amongst others.

Of her brothers, Suniti Devi was very attached to the oldest, Karuna (to whom she was closest in age), a religious man who carried on his father's

Nirmala Sen, Nilina's mother

LEFT Saral and Nirmala Sen and four of their children. Sunith (at the back), Nilina and Sadhona (left and right), baby Prodeep

work. He was helped by his wife, who copied many of their father's prayers and became a teacher in the Victoria College when it needed teachers. And while she was fond of all her brothers, two others were very special to her. One was Profullo, who was her 'most affectionate little friend' and became the favourite uncle of her children until his death. The other was the fourth brother, Saral. According to some, Keshub Chandra's great gifts and spiritual devotion were inherited by Saral, who was loved as a kind-hearted and unselfish individual by his sister; indeed, many thought he would become a missionary like his father. When Suniti Devi's husband, the Maharaja, lay ill with the pneumonia which was eventually to prove fatal, it was Saral who nursed him day and night. The last words that the Maharaja wrote were on a slip of paper: only two words: 'Saral . . . household.' Very probably he wished this brother to take care of his wife, such was his confidence in him.

And indeed, after their mother, Jaganmohini Devi, had passed away, the sisters who remained single lived at Lily Cottage with Saral, who looked after them with great tenderness until they were married. In her autobiography, Suniti Devi quoted him as saying: 'Unless my sisters marry I shall remain single, and I shall not accept any post that will take me away from them.' But, of course, he did marry, and continued to stay on in Lily Cottage. His wife, Nirmala, also called Nellie, came from a distinguished family of lawyers; her father, Purna Chandra Sen, was the Advocate General of Burma and one of her younger brothers, A.K. Sen, was a Judge of the Calcutta High Court.

Nilina (far right) with her Guru, Girija Shankar Chakravarty

Nilina Sen

It was Saral and Nellie who were the parents of Nilina, their second youngest child and youngest daughter. Their other four children were two sons, Sunit and Prodeep, and two daughters, Benita and Sadhona.

At first glance they appeared like opposites. Saral was a gentle soul, a thorough gentleman and a good lawyer who had studied for the Bar in England, but he was not particularly outgoing. Nellie was sparkling and feisty, a 'beautiful firebrand', as someone described her. She had a strong

sense of humour, a quality inherited by all her children, and their home was filled with laughter. Like all strong personalities she had a quick temper; equally she was warm-hearted and just as quick to forget. Most of all, for her husband and children she was the rock and pivot of the family, its soul and strength, from whom they all drew sustenance. It was a household where, despite the age differences between the siblings, there were bonds of closeness and deep affection. Each of the three daughters lived lives that described exceptional trajectories and followed very different paths in very different places. Yet they unfolded their talents to each other when they were children to collaborate in creative projects, and called themselves the Besani sisters. Benita was the playwright, the poet, the story teller who wrote the scripts to be acted out; Sadhona, exquisitely beautiful even at that tender age, would dance; and Nilina, with her innate gift for music, would sing. It was like a glimpse into the future, certainly into the lives that Sadhona and Nilina would eventually lead.

Such activities flowed from the nurturing climate of the home, the ever present music, the songs that Saral and Nelly sang as they played on piano and violin, and the many soirees held in the house by Nilina's adored older brother, Sunith, where musicians like Enayat Khan, Mehdi Husain Khan and Girija Shankar Chakravarty would participate in intimate *baithaks*. One such *baithak* sparked the start of her learning process when she was a little girl; as Girija Babu ended his performance, he asked her what she had liked best. 'Your Bhairavi,' she replied, referring to the *thumri* that he had just concluded. 'Can you sing it for me?' he asked. She sang it; and such was her confidence and her clarity that he made her his pupil on the spot. She learned from him for the next nine years, before the long silence of the next phase of her life began.

It was Benita, Saral and Nellie's second child and oldest daughter (she was almost a decade older than Nilina) who followed the footsteps of her aunts, Suniti Devi and Sucharu Devi, by marrying the Chakma Raja whose capital, Rangamati, was located to the east, in the Chittagong Hill Tracts. On the surface this was a most unlikely wedding; many people in Calcutta did not even know who the Chakmas were or where they lived; it was like venturing into some exotic terra incognita. The Chakma chiefdom was, like Cooch Behar and Mayurbhanj, a mainly tribal area; its people were believed to have come from the Arakan area of Myanmar to settle in these hills, where they cultivated rice and bamboo and practiced a version of Theravada Buddhism. Benita herself, a bright student and scholarship winner at Bethune College, might not have been the most eager of brides, yet her future father-in-law was very keen that his sons marry educated girls from enlightened families and her lineage and credentials were impeccable. All this seemed to echo a familiar pattern initiated by Keshub Chandra Sen himself and followed by his daughters, a call for bringing development to remote areas and opening up access to education. The Chakma Raja Nalinaksha Roy, with the help of his wife, undertook reforms in education. Rani Benita, under the patronage of her close friend Rabindranath Tagore, launched *Garika*, the first literary magazine to feature poetry in the Chakma language.

Rani Benita Roy of the Chakma Raj, Nilina's oldest sister

Benita's commitment to her people endured the most unexpected twists and turns of fortune. The first came in 1947 with Partition, when a stroke of the pen placed the Buddhist majority Hill Tracts in the predominantly Muslim East Pakistan (now Bangladesh). A few years later, Benita's son, Tridiv Roy, ascended the *gaddi* as Raja and the second major change occurred when the Kaptai Dam was built on the Karnaphuli River, resulting in the displacement of thousands of people and the loss of a sizable area of arable land for farming. The Chakma Palace too went under water, and was replaced by a new one built in in 1960.

But the most significant change, and the one that inexorably divided mother and son, took place in 1971 with the Liberation War in East Pakistan and the subsequent formation of Bangladesh. In this conflict, both were compelled to make choices and take sides. Benita Roy chose to remain with the Chakmas and Bangladesh and made her preference known by opening up the Rangamati Palace to affected civilians; Tridiv Roy opted to side with Pakistan, where he went and stayed for the rest of his life. He feared that in Bangladesh the Chakmas would be reduced to a minority in their own homelands; consequently he never returned to Rangamati, not even for a visit, though he steadfastly remained a Buddhist until he passed away.

Both held offices in their respective countries as Government Ministers; but a dramatic high point was reached at the United Nations in 1972 when the delegations of Bangladesh and Pakistan arrived, the former to request admission to the UN and the latter to request that such admission be denied. Tridiv Roy and his mother were members of their respective national delegations; it was reported that Bangladeshi Prime Minister Mujib-ur-Rehman had specially sent Benita to persuade her son to come back to Bangladesh but that he refused to do so. This poignant story of the assertion of identity on the one hand being pitted against the fear of its loss on the other is one of those examples of truth being far stranger than fiction.

All this was, of course, far into the future. At the time that Benita got married to the Chakma Raja Nalinaksha Roy, Nilina was not even ten years old and one consequence of this wedding was that the relationship between her and Sadhona became even closer. It was as if they were twin souls, joined at the hip, who laughed and enjoyed the same things and were gifted by a familial and natural talent for the arts. In this they were encouraged by their parents who viewed the cultivation of music and dance as a part of a liberal education, a private and inward flowering of the personality, never ever meant for showing in public. The girls went to school at the Victoria Institute established by their grandfather, and wherever Sadhona went, Nilina would follow, an adoring acolyte of her older sister.

'Exquisite' was the word most often used to describe Sadhona even when she was a child, a word that recurred endlessly in connection with the graceful movements of her body, the limpid fluidity of her wrists and gestures of her hands, the eloquence of her eyes: she was a born dancer who had trained in Kathak with Taraknath Bagchi and Manipuri dance with Guru Senarik Rajkumar. Along with Nilina, she too had learnt music from Girija Babu, though she lacked Nilina's patience, chafing at the countless times her purist guru made her repeat the notes of the raga. 'I can't go on singing "*Mudri mori kahe ko cheen li..*" for another two years!' she would rage to Nilina.

Sadhona Bose, Nilina's sister, glamorous actress and dancer

Girija Shankar Chakravarty was indeed a perfectionist who lived and breathed in an atmosphere soaked in music. Though he had tried his hand successfully at both acting and painting, his true calling was music, much to the chagrin of his father, a well-known lawyer, who wanted his son to follow his profession. Earning a living through music was not regarded with esteem amongst the upper middle classes. Yet nothing could stop Girija Babu in the single minded pursuit of his passion, and when he dedicated himself solely to music it was under the tutelage of Radhika Prasad Goswami, court musician of the Raja of Kasimbazar, from whom he learnt the majestic forms of *dhrupad* and *dhamar*. A little later, he stayed for a while in Calcutta with Shyamlal Khettri, an eminent patron and seeker of music, whose house was always open as a home for promising young musicians. Two of his fellow guests were legendary for their command over *thumri*; one was Bhaiyasahib Ganpat Rao, the harmonium wizard who wrote *thumris* under the pen name of Sughara

Priya, and whose skill in the genre was said to be unparalleled. The other was his student, Moizuddin Khan, whose sweet haunting voice gave him the title of Badshah of *Thumri*. Girija Babu was quick to become a pupil of Bhaiyasahib Ganpat Rao and learnt much also from Moizuddin Khan.

As an eager student, distance was no deterrent to learning, he travelled to Delhi and later, to Rampur, then an acknowledged centre of music, thanks to the patronage of the Nawab of Rampur. Here he studied the nuances of khayal gayaki with Ustad Enayat Husain Khan, and his education in khayal continued when he returned to Calcutta and learnt with the ageing maestro, Ustad Badal Khan.

Girija Babu was acknowledged as not only a great singer who had perfected his technique in all the major genres of Hindustani music, learning from masters of different gharanas, but also a great teacher. As his students, Nilina and Sadhona were in good company—his other pupils included the great flautist Pannalal Ghosh and the singers A. Kanan and Sunil Bose. Having gone through an arduous learning process himself, it is understandable that he would accept nothing less from his own pupils. Equally, it is perhaps understandable that Sadhona, whose interest lay primarily in dance, might not appreciate his intense style of teaching, though her own love of music was unquestionable.

Perhaps it was at this stage that *thumri*, transmitted to Nilina through the true masters of the art, so captivated her imagination and her heart that the genre and its range became her life-long musical focus. There was something about the form and its variants that was utterly alluring and irresistible, both for its intrinsic musical challenges as well as its expressions of femininity. It was one of the mainstays in the repertoire of the *tawaif* or *baiji*, the professional woman singers. Their music was heard everywhere: in private performances held in the homes of the wealthy to celebrate births, weddings, or special family occasions; in the theatres of Calcutta for the many Bengali operas and musical dramas that were so popular; and—more and more often—in the 'new media' of that era, namely recording and film. The recording industry created stars and launched singers like Gauhar Jaan into national fame. In many ways it democratized that music, and broadened the listener base by making it accessible to a much larger number of people.

Nilina, however, had the opportunity to listen in person to one of the biggest singing stars, the legendary Angurbala who was a performer across many platforms. She was a stage actress with a charismatic presence, a recording star who later also appeared in films. She had learnt the art of *thumri* from Ram Prasad Mishra and Ustad Jamiruddin Khan, and she was also acknowledged as a leading artiste in the rendition of Nazrul geeti, the compositions of the maverick poet Kazi Nazrul Islam, whose original and creative expressions also embraced short stories, plays, film directing and film music. Angurbala thought of him as a creative genius who had a unique way of working. Sometimes he would just explain the notations of the song, then turn to her and say, 'Angur, it's now up to you to add the sweet *angur* (grape) flavour of your voice.' That sweet voice travelled south all the way to Hyderabad where the Nizam himself was enchanted by it, and specially invited her to perform at his court.

When she was a young girl, one of Nilina's uncles took her to see Angurbala perform at the Minerva Theatre; and she was completely entranced by the singing, the unfolding narrative, the costumes: in short, the total magic of theatre. So enraptured was she by the ravishing Angurbala that the sympathetic uncle took her to the singer's house to meet her. Little Nilina was treated kindly and invited to sing, and when she had finished her song, she in turn asked Angurbala to sing for her, which she did. It was an altogether dazzling experience for the child; for Angurbala, perhaps the high clear notes of Nilina's song brought back bittersweet memories of her own deprived and impoverished childhood when she had to leave her home and abandon her education to learn singing and earn a living. Seeing the girl's innocence, she must have recognized that the uncle should not have brought her there, Nilina should not even be in her home; it was not acceptable for females of respectable families to be in the company of women who earned their livelihoods through professional singing. No, another such meeting with this charming child was not going to be possible; instead, she gave Nilina her telephone number and invited her to call whenever she wished,

so that Angurbala could sing her a song. This was an irresistible invitation and exploited to the fullest by Nilina and Sadhona who would giggle as they dialed her number to listen to her magic voice, dreaming of the day when they too could be star performers on a stage, little comprehending that this was a path forbidden to them.

But for Sadhona, that *was* her path. Perhaps there was an element of precociousness in the young Sadhona, a desire to achieve too much too soon, to become a great artiste in her own right as fast as possible. And then, when she was just a teenager, the director Modhu Bose became a significant presence in her life and changed it forever. He was the son of a family friend, the distinguished geologist Pramatha Natha Bose who discovered huge iron ore deposits for the Tata Iron & Steel Company and whose statue still stands in front of their factory in Jamshedpur. Modhu had entered the world of film as an actor but then assisted directors like J.J. Madan and Himanshu Rai. In the mid-1920s he worked abroad honing his camera techniques and working for directors like Fritz Lang. He shot a Burmese film for the London film Company in Rangoon, then returned to Calcutta to start a theatre group.

He was, of course, much older than Sadhona and Nilina; ironically, at first they used to call him Modhu Mama. Both girls performed as part of the chorus for his stage production of *Ali Baba*. Given the social conventions of the time, we have to wonder how Saral Sen and his wife even allowed this. Two possible reasons emerge—one, that Modhu's father and Saral's father were close friends, thus they were confident that this was a known party that they were dealing with; and two, that it was Modhu Bose's declared intention to 'clean up theatre' by putting on the stage young ladies of good family.

But by then, and having heard him sing in his deep and melodious voice, Sadhona was totally smitten and wanted to marry him. She was much too young; at that point he was twice her age; the family was appalled and tried to forbid the marriage; but had to retreat reluctantly in the face of her determination. She made herself sick, literally, and kept falling sick until her parents consented to the match. It was a case of extreme infatuation and hero worship, an innocent teenager's romantic and appealing notion of life shared with the artistically creative Modhu, someone to be admired and who could magically open all kinds of doors for her. And eventually they married in 1930.

Sadhona Bose in her most famous film role as *Raj Nartaki* (The Court Dancer)

After her marriage she performed as leading lady on stage, including *Ali Baba* where she now shifted to the prominent role of Marjina; and in 1933, she acted as Ameena in *Dalia*, a production based on the short story by Rabindranath Tagore which, it is recorded, the great poet himself both supervised and attended. Success came with *Ali Baba*, the film version made in 1937, directed by Modhu Bose, where Sadhona reprised her stage role of Marjina. The film was a huge hit, followed by another successful film, *Abhinoy*, after which they moved to Bombay (now Mumbai). Then, in 1941, came the film that has defined Sadhona Bose for generations of film lovers—*Raj Nartaki* (The Court Dancer). It was also the film which became the reference point for Nilina as the apex of cinematic achievement of her beloved sister, Sadhona Bose, her *mejdi*.

In many ways, this was an audacious venture: the first film made in India in three languages, English, Bengali and Hindi. It was a coup pulled off by the redoubtable J.B.H. Wadia of Wadia Movietone who proudly claimed it as the first Indian film with dialogues in English made by an Indian crew. To this achievement he added a stellar cast and crew which included matinee idol Prithviraj Kapoor as the hero, Timir Baran as the music composer, Modhu Bose as director and scriptwriter and Manmatha Ray for the story. The film's credits also listed Sadhona Bose as the costume designer. Other credits were quite intriguing: the distinguished anthropologist, Verrier Elwin, was acknowledged as the translator of songs into English. Mediaman D.F. Karaka supplied 'suggestions'. There was no credit for choreography,

but, given the period, we may quite logically assume that it was Sadhona herself, just as we may assume (in the absence of credits) that the singing was hers.

The story was set in early 19th century Manipur and centered around the ill-fated love story of a prince and a court dancer destined never to be together because of her 'low' status as a mere dancer. Eventually she sacrifices herself; she takes poison and dies in his arms. Amongst the film's many highlights are the choreography and an extraordinary and lovely Wadia special-effects touch to illustrate how the hand movements of the dance (executed by Sadhona with perfect grace) represent the stars and the moon. It was a huge hit, much of which we may credit to the delicate and luminous beauty of its female lead and her dancing skills as well as the spectacular scenes and sets.

But what followed in Sadhona's questing life never seemed to match the brilliance of that accomplishment even though she established herself as a heroine in her own right in major films like *Shankar Parvati*, *Vishkanya*, and *Paigham*. She was no longer as dependent on Modhu, indeed, she was now more famous than him, a star in her own right, and inevitably that put the marriage under strain. They were two highly talented people with egos to match, and their strong personalities led to inevitable clashes, making their relationship ever more destructive. She was also very highly-strung. Somewhere during this period she turned to alcohol to soothe her restless nerves and disappointed expectations and soon developed an addiction which was the beginning of a downward spiral and a very tragic end. The film world, then as now, was very competitive, there were other actresses such as the beautiful Devika Rani (a grand-niece of Tagore) and Kanan Bala. The film offers started drying up, but performance was in Sadhona's blood and she formed a dance troupe to present productions choreographed by her with boldness yet respect for the rules of the form: *Ajanta; Bhookh* (Hunger), her instinctive and creative political response to the terrible famine in Bengal which she expressed in Bharatanatyam and which was lauded as 'the most extraordinary concept in dance'; and *Abhisar*, which was based on the poem of Rabindranath Tagore, where she played the role of the dancer Vasavdatta.

In the latter half of the 1940s she undertook dance productions for the Indian Revival Group led by Yog Sunder, one of which, Birth of Freedom, was a one-hour ballet which echoed the national mood of a newly independent India. She danced as Mother India to cheering audiences against a backdrop of tableaux of scenes from the Freedom struggle. A few years later she formed a group in Bombay, the New Age Dancers which, unfortunately, faded away after a few performances in Bombay and Calcutta.

But by now she was now caught in the relentless grip of her addiction and was reduced to unhappy circumstances, so different from the high life of earlier years. Gone were the Bentley cars, her opulent homes in Bombay and Calcutta. Towards the end, her life was confined to a bleak apartment in Calcutta which she shared with her husband until he died: two brilliant, once-famous people in a seedy one-room flat. For a woman of such great talent who had achieved so much in her life, had become such an icon, this was a very sad end. By this time, Nilina had left her childhood and Lily Cottage far behind. She was half-way across the country, a sad, long-distance witness to the deterioration of a beloved sister whom she had always admired as a genius in her art. Her sorrow was silent, she kept the raw emotion of that wound within herself, choosing not to talk about it, remembering instead only the happy times, the music and the laughter.

But her deepest feelings emerged many years later in 1973 when Sadhona passed away. However tormented her life had been, she had once won the hearts of millions with her creative spirit, her enormous talent, her grace and extraordinary beauty. She could not let her sister's death go unmarked without a poignant and loving tribute, and a few months later she participated in a memorial programme at the Kala Mandir in Calcutta. For the performance she turned to the young Kathak dancer, Shovana Narayan, who had briefly been a student of Sadhona's, and invited her to recreate two items from her early repertoire of the late 1930s or early 1940s, *Omar*

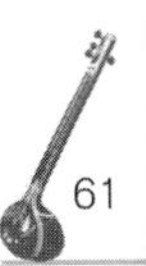

Khayyam and *Street Dancer*. Shovana had to re-work the choreography based on a copy of the original script of the former. For her, this first choreography was a vital learning experience in the totality of presentation, right from opening one's mind to interpretations of content to more practical things like the selection of costumes and music. And her reward reminded her of how strong that intangible bond between the sisters had remained till the last. From Sadhona's dancing *ghungroos*, two were placed in her palm by Nilina, by then known as Naina Devi, who said: 'Take these, this is your *gurudakshina* from her'. Of course this was a reversal of the concept where it is the student who offers and the guru who accepts. But it was Naina Devi's way of keeping alive a small and precious flame of memory.

When Sadhona married Modhu Bose in 1930, it left Nilina and Prodeep as the two children remaining in Lily Cottage. At this time one might imagine that Saral and Nellie Sen were concerned about the future of their youngest daughter who was showing perhaps a bit too much of a love for music, a dangerous propensity in view of what had happened. At that moment fate intervened and a chance meeting (though is any meeting ever chance?) propelled Nilina to the next phase of her life.

In the way of all societies, one's connections and acquaintances were freely shared with one's friends, especially those who were visiting a new city. It so happened that Kanwar Ripjit Singh, the son of Raja Charanjit Singh of the royal house of Kapurthala, had accompanied his sister, Pamela, to Calcutta where she had gone to shop for her trousseau. She was engaged to Jyoti Prasada, the son of Jwala Prasada, a very eminent zamindar of Shahjahanpur in Uttar Pradesh who was also an officer of the Imperial Civil Service (ICS). His wife, Jyoti's mother, was Bengali, in fact, her maiden name was Sudakshana, which was changed to Purnima after her marriage, and she was the youngest daughter of Hemendranath Tagore. This marriage was the first recorded instance of a lady from a prominent family of Bengal marrying into a family in Uttar Pradesh. It was Jyoti, Pamela's fiancé, who wrote to Ripjit Singh to suggest that he call on Mrs Sen, the daughter-in-law of Keshub Chandra Sen, and her family, which included a daughter with

Nilina Sen

a beautiful singing voice. The closeness between the Sens and the Tagores was well known, and Ripjit Singh was warmly received as the brother of Pamela, Purnima Tagore Prasada's future daughter-in-law.

Nilina came to join the group, a demure young presence in a simple pink sari with her hair left open. Ripjit Singh asked her to sing: perhaps he was curious about that beautiful singing voice. Of course Nilina responded immediately with one of her favourite songs: all she ever needed was an excuse to sing! In that moment, and as he heard her sing, he was bewitched by the sweetness of her voice, as he was indeed entranced by the grace of that petite form and her gentle innocence. He was instantly and completely certain that this was the girl he wanted to marry; and it took him no time at all to place the proposal before Nilina's parents and declare that he would not leave Calcutta until the wedding had taken place.

It must have been quite a dilemma for them and they thought it over very carefully. On the one hand, there was Nilina's young age and a family whose home was a place that was thousands of kilometers away. On the other, there

was Sadhona, already a presence on the Calcutta stage and heading toward stardom, a major influence on her sister who idolized her, whose example they did not want their youngest daughter to emulate. With her passion for music it was quite possible that Nilina, too, might be adamant in opting for a performer's life. It was a possibility they had to remove, and here was an opportunity for them to do so. After all, the proposal had come from a prominent and wealthy family of very distinguished lineage in the Punjab; the suitor was a most presentable young man who clearly was serious about her and would look after her and keep her happy. Eventually it made sense for them to accept his proposal.

And what about Nilina herself? Certainly she was very young by the standards of our times, but then that was altogether a different era. There were no options to marriage for a well-brought-up girl of good family, and she would be following her aunts and sister in marrying into a family of royal blood. Though she had to leave behind the security and familiar warmth of home and parents and the contacts of good friends, such as the Tagores of the Jorasanko Thakurbadi, she had the good fortune to have a bridegroom who would remain devoted to her for the rest of his life and with whom she was to share much happiness. In any event, things moved forward with breathless haste, for there were only two weeks between the acceptance of the proposal and the wedding itself, which left little time to brood over the future.

In this interim, there was one important matter to be resolved: Ripjit Singh's father had to be asked for his consent to the wedding; it would have been inconceivable to take such a major step without seeking his approval and his blessings. This was not easily forthcoming. Raja Charanjit Singh was not at all pleased with the idea. His objections to the match are not known, but he must have surely hesitated at the thought of a bride he had never met coming from so far away. However, Ripjit Singh stood firm and at last received a rather curt telegram from his father in which he was told that he was given the consent but not the blessings. This was a message that was singularly lacking in love or charm, yet was very characteristic of the Raja for its precise clarity.

But meanwhile there was a wedding to be organized and celebrated. Even in that short span of time, Saral and Nellie Sen managed a host of grand functions attended by the elite of Calcutta and beyond. Members of royal families from Bengal and Orissa, some of whom were Nilina's family members, and from that of Awadh, who had a profound connection with Ripjit Singh's grandfather, were present to offer their felicitations and their best wishes. There was a recital by the famous dhrupad maestro, Pandit Ram Chatur Mallick, the last court musican of the Darbhanga Raj.

Throughout her life, it was the haunting strains of that voice which remained one of her most abiding memories of the moments when she made the transition from Nilina Sen to Rani Nina Ripjit Singh.

RANI NINA RIPJIT SINGH

SIMLA, RAJANAGAR, DELHI, AWADH: 1935–1953

From Nilina to Nina

It is not recorded how soon after their marriage Nilina and Kanwar Ripjit Singh set off for his home, but the assumption is that the bridegroom lost little time in taking his bride away. There is no record, either, of whether Nilina was frightened or nervous; at the young age of 18, her life was about to change forever under unfamiliar circumstances, with no one close to her to whom she could turn for help, though there was, for the moment, her soon-to-be-married sister-in-law, Pamela.

It was a long journey heading west by train from Calcutta to Simla across the Indo-Gangetic plains. Of course by the mid-1930s this had become a well-worn track, established almost a hundred years ago and reinforced six decades ago when the full splendour of the British Raj and its offices ranging from viceroy to peons began their annual trek to their summer headquarters in the hills. But in 1935 as the bridal couple made their way towards Ambala and Kalka, the solitude and privacy of the long journey gave them a chance to get to know each other better and forged the bond between them that would end only with his death. Throughout their marriage his support and affection, indeed his adoration, was what sustained her during difficult times and eased the pain of separation from her own family, the wrench of not hearing the sweet rounded syllables of Bengali, the alien taste of bland Western food without spices, and the sad lack of music in her life.

Meanwhile, as the couple reached Kalka, they had to change trains to make the final leg of their journey to Simla. The narrow gauge railway was a marvel of engineering which managed the ascent from Kalka at a little over 2,100 feet to Simla at well over 7,000 feet, through a series of loops and tight

Kalka-Simla Railway, a passenger train on one of the smaller bridges

curves, winding its way over bridges that looked like Roman aqueducts and cutting through more than one hundred tunnels. The air grew fresher as they ascended, and the fragrance of pines stronger; and surely no railway station could be prettier than that at Barog with its 'flower gardens with fountains and running water'. And finally, after admiring spectacular views of the mountains, they arrived in Simla, where one of the people to welcome her was the young Sharda, daughter of Kanwar Sir Jagdish Prasad of Moradabad, a distinguished Member of the Viceroy's Executive Council. At that early meeting no one could imagine that it would lead to an enduring friendship that lasted through Nilina's life and shaped her destiny in a remarkable manner. But now it was time to go to Chadwick for her first meeting with Ripjit's father, Raja Charanjit Singh.

Surely she must have wondered about a father-in-law who had given consent grudgingly, and had so coldly and gracelessly withheld his blessings. This was completely unlike the family she came from where emotions escaped like steam from a kettle; but, in the end, all was warmth, all was love. Doubtless Ripjit Singh described to her the home they were going to, the superbly

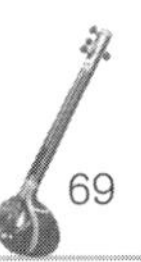

elegant Chadwick, poised on one of the spurs of Summerhill and one of the most gracious residences in all of Simla. And in his enthusiastic recounting of the new life they would share, he must have also communicated his own deep love for his father.

A portrait of Raja Charanjit Singh

Raja Charanjit Singh was an enigmatic figure held in awe by his family and feared by most of them. A photograph taken by the Lafayette Studio of London when he was on a visit there in 1920 shows a man whose presence is calm and regal. He sits poised with confidence wearing a lustrous brocade achkan and a turban on which is mounted an elaborate *sarpech*; and though the picture is in black and white there is no mistaking the intricate ornamentation of the jewel and its fine craftsmanship in gold and gemstones. Upon his chest are some of the many medals he was awarded: the Durbar Medals of 1903 and 1911 and the Coronation Medal of the same year. He exudes an indefinable aura which comes from being a member of the Royal house of Kapurthala. In this family, when litigation between brothers had occurred, it was sorted out by the award of monies and properties, which created collateral branches of significance and great wealth, making each of them distinct, yet powerful, entities. The Raja was the son of one such branch. His access to people in high places is borne out by an entry in the London Court Circular of 9th June 1920: 'Sirdar Charanjit Singh of Kapurthala gave a dinner party at Claridges Hotel last night to meet the Secretary of State for India and Mrs Montagu. The Sirdar proposed a toast to their health in a short speech to which Mr Montagu responded.'

But somewhere in his heart there was an icy splinter and it came from rejection and the lack of paternal love in his childhood. Raja Charanjit Singh was the son of Kanwar Suchet Singh, the youngest brother of the ruler, Raja Randhir

Singh. Suchet Singh—as was accepted in those times—had a wife (Charanjit's mother) as well as two 'second wives' or concubines, Muslim ladies who each bore him a son. In the typical manner of that era, they might have been high-born but lesser valued ladies drawn from a complex and tragic social circumstance of surplus women. It was the latter two and their sons who became the prime objects of Suchet Singh's affections and were given much attention and importance. The wife and her son (born when Suchet Singh was in his forties) were relegated to the background and more-or-less ignored. That sense of being ignored despite his legitimate claims must have permeated his youth and his outlook, for it affected his psyche forever. His half-brothers were loved and well-educated at the prestigious Aitchison College in Lahore; he was sent to Jullunder (now Jalandhar). It was a deprivation during his formative years of many things he felt were due to him, and created a sense of isolation and insecurity. It was only when he was 17 years old that his father sent for him. At that time Suchet Singh lay on his deathbed and was keenly aware of his own mortality, perhaps aware also of the possibility of endless lawsuits between all his sons over the family wealth and property. He clasped Charanjit's hand, then placed it in his physician's hand declaring, 'This is my son and my heir.'

Kanwar Suchet Singh, father of Raja Charanjit Singh, known as Bade Sarkar

We can only imagine the bitterness that flooded the young boy's heart at this acknowledgement: too little, too late, how the recollection of all those wasted years must have stung. It is difficult to offer love when none has been given you, and the shadow and sadness of those early years of neglect translated into a strict discipline that was imposed, very often with undue harshness. And with a formality that was part a reflection of the current hierarchical social mores and part the instinctive thrusting away of any form

of intimacy. So it was that his own son, Ripjit, called him Sarkar: only that, not Daddy or Papa or Pitaji. In conversation it was *Jee Hazur, Jee Sarkar*, a cold and arm's length distance of courtesy.

This is all the more surprising—or perhaps, given his persona, it is not—because Ripjit Singh was in fact his third son and now the only one with whom he had any contact. Charanjit Singh's relationship with his two older sons, Rajkumar Ajit Singh and Rajkumar Sarabjit Singh, boys who were a year apart in age, had come to a total halt at some point well before Nilina arrived in Simla. The reason for this estrangement was never clearly established, or it may be that this was yet another family feud whose beginnings were lost in the mists of speculation and rumour. But until the rift occurred, he had been a caring young father who wanted to give his sons all the advantages he felt that he himself had not been given: Ajit Singh was educated at Harrow and Sarabjit Singh at Eton. The cause remains a puzzle. Was there a perceived insult? Had his sons, upon whom he had doted, to whom he had given generously of himself and his resources, turned against him or made undue demands? Had Charanjit Singh's ear, highly vulnerable and sensitive to slight, been poisoned by an interested party? It would seem so; and that the problem centred around the mother of the boys and an insult allegedly heaped upon her by her sons. Whether this was correct or not, the matter was conveyed to Charanjit Singh by his wife's brother, the uncle of the boys, perhaps subtly repeated until it became a dark truth. His motive for doing so was not immediately clear; maybe he feared the loss of his own closeness and importance to Charanjit Singh once the sons were more actively on the scene, a loss of control precipitated by their growing independence, a dimunition of his own light.

Whatever the reason, it led to an abrupt ending of relations; and when that cut came, it was swift and brutal, the instant disassociation with his two sons reflecting the depth of the hurt Charanjit Singh felt. It was like a mirror image of the rejection of his own childhood. He never met them or spoke to them again. Even when his wife, their mother, passed away in Delhi and they asked permission to come to pay their respects, the bitter answer, as he denied them, was: 'What respects?'

We may marvel at the utter steeliness of a man who could so cold-bloodedly sever himself from his own children, apparently without a backward look. But we should also wonder whether he ever gave a thought to the aftermath and the consequences: the third son and the daughter who never knew their brothers, the mother separated from her sons. These were the heavy prices paid by others for his deep insecurity and misguided sense of pride. Only much, much later was the uncle's role uncovered and by then it had ceased to matter.

Rani Sahiba, wife of Raja sahib and mother of Kanwar Ripjit Singh

Nilina, now addressed as Nina, may or may not have known any of this at that time. But her sensitivity must have alerted her to the fact that Ripjit and his father had quite a different relationship to the one she enjoyed with her own parents. With this perception she arrived in Chadwick, which was in Summerhill, a suburb of Simla that even had its own railway station. And she was finally face to face with Raja Charanjit Singh.

He had never been in favour of this marriage to an unknown girl from so far away; his own preference would have been for a Punjabi princess or at the very least a high-born girl from an aristocratic family of land-owners. But part of his hostility melted away as he saw the petite, pretty figure in front of him, clearly a well-brought-up and well-spoken person of politeness and refinement. She seemed to be intelligent, adaptable and graceful, a malleable social asset whom he could shape into a most presentable official hostess for himself. It was a very pleasant surprise, a bonus he had not expected, a need fulfilled as his own daughter's marriage was only a few months away. Instinctively he sensed that she would never contradict him nor go against his wishes, and that her youth was an advantage that would help her integrate seamlessly into his family.

Nina and Chadwick

In 1935 when Nina arrived in Simla, the Second World War was still a few years away and Simla was a large town, the summer capital of a vast country, a town illuminated by a sense of its own importance and by the magnetic ebb and flow of its inhabitants who came and went in an established annual ritual.

Its beginnings lay—as such things so often do—in its geography, when two pioneering officers of the East India Company undertook a survey in 1817 to map the hill states and noticed how the Sutlej Valley provided a natural highway that connected the Punjab to the plateau of Western Tibet. Their interest was instantly sparked by this discovery. From Tibet came, amongst many other valuable goods, the precious pashm wool, the soft fleece of the neck and underbelly of the ibex, used for the hand-woven shawls which were much in demand. For centuries, Kashmir was the only place where these fine shawls could be made, thanks to treaties that gave the Maharaja of Kashmir exclusive rights to Tibet's pashmina supply; and to the complex processes that the women of Kashmir had perfected over generations to create the lightest, warmest wool. Beyond this lay an enormous commercial benefit: 'Next to diamonds and laces, sometimes even before either, ladies love cashmere shawls,' a British magazine breathlessly reported, reflecting the European craze for shawls and a thriving export market.

The potential value made this a business opportunity not to be missed, something the Company Bahadur wanted to seize as a monopoly. It was possible that the raw wool and other goods could come directly into British hands if an alternate route bypassing Kashmir could be opened up, for example through Bushahr, where Rampur was already a thriving entrepôt for goods from Tibet, Yarkhand and Ladakh. Simla was conveniently located on the existing trade link between Rampur in Bushahr and Sirsa in the plains, a route which was open for six months in the year.

There was, however, a problem. The hill states were controlled by the Gurkhas who had built forts to establish their sway over the area. They also controlled the passes to Tibet and the trade, and did not allow foreigners to trade, effectively shutting out the East India Company from any possibility of lucrative deals. This situation was dealt with by simply taking over the forts through military action; once the Gurkhas were defeated, the hill states territories were re-aligned and parcelled out by the British. The former rulers were reinstated; finely-tuned adjustments were made, depending on who had helped to vanquish the Gurkhas (Patiala, for instance, gained portions of the confiscated territories) and some of the forts were retained. Conditions were applied to the newly-restored rulers: they had to build roads and supply labour under an iniquitous system called *begaree*, amongst other demands. The hill people, described as 'a docile population with submissive hill rulers', accepted these demands and got on with their lives.

Amidst all this action, the Simla ridge became a popular hunting area, so much so that the Assistant Political Agent, Lt. Ross, built a thatched cottage to accommodate enthusiasts of this sport. His successor, Lt. Kennedy, added a gabled cottage, Kennedy House, which became the first permanent structure of the town. As Agent, Kennedy wielded substantial power and was a key figure in the growth of the new town. Just a few years later the Governor General, Lord Amherst, arrived for his first stay, a sojourn of two months, accompanied by a large entourage. By the time he left, six large houses had been built for this group; and by 1830, the British presence had been firmly established with 30 houses dotting lands acquired from the princes who had been compensated in the land swop. Simla was now a small town of six square miles set amidst the hill states. Its status as an established hill station was cemented by the visit of the Governor General, Lord Bentinck, in 1831; by the mid-19th century there were 100 houses and a steady British population catered to by hotels, boarding houses and a club. It was maturing into a place where the British could live in a cool, fresh climate and in an environment where they could create a sense of being back home in their own country.

The growth of Simla was speeded up by events in the Punjab. Its location and relative proximity to the plains made it an ideal place for soldiers

convalescing in the aftermath of two Anglo-Sikh wars. It was also a strategic base from where men and arms could be speedily advanced to battle areas. And when, after the death of Maharaja Ranjit Singh, the whole of the Punjab erupted into chaos, it was only a matter of time before his erstwhile empire fell into the hands of the British. During this time they tightened their grip on the town by surrounding it with cantonments strategically placed in Dagshai, Solan and Kasauli like a protective ring around Simla.

Maharaja Ranjit Singh, 1830, painted by Leopold Massard

Both before and after the death of Maharaja Ranjit Singh, the Punjab remained a focus of British interest. Successive Governors General came on tours to northern India and included Simla on their visits; Auckland, whose attempt to resolve the Afghan issue led to a residence of two years in Simla and who arrived accompanied by a minor army of staff and secretaries; Ellenborough; and Hardinge. Dalhousie spent three consecutive summers in Simla during the annexation of the Punjab, and he it was who thought up a plan for a Grand Hindustan-Tibet Road to start from Kalka that would forever guarantee safe passage for trade between the two areas. But by now, trade had become a secondary issue.

Upto this point, apart from its development as a community residence for the British, the town of Simla remained a convenient centre point surrounded by sanatoriums for convalescents and military cantonments. It was not yet the summer capital of the Raj, not yet an annual feature. Soon, however, as one historian puts it: 'While in 1814, Ochterlony had wondered how an elephant could be transported through the hills, half a century later, the Simla hills were ready to receive another elephant, a large white one – the Government of India offices and its staff.'

Quite clearly, for some years circumstances had been moving towards formalizing Simla as the summer capital of the Raj. After all, the provinces already made similar moves—the Madras Government shifted

Sir John Lawrence,
1st Baron Lawrence, c. 1895

to Ootacamund, Bombay Government went to Mahabaleshwar, and so on. But in this case, both the sheer expense and the distance that caused daunting logistics seemed to defeat attempts to formalize the move. Now the decision was precipitated by the appointment of John Lawrence as Viceroy in the mid-1860s. Indeed, Lawrence agreed to take up this office conditional to being able to operate from Simla during the summer months, quoting ill health as his reason; certainly he was a person who knew the area well, for he was an experienced Punjab hand, having served in the province as Administrator and later, Chief Commissioner. In addition Lawrence offered strong arguments to support his demand: '...Here you are with one foot, I may say, in the Punjab, and another in the North-West Provinces. Here you are among a docile population, and yet near enough to influence Awadh...' It was a clear outline of strategic British priorities in a post-1857 scenario and surely weighed the scales in favour of Simla and Lawrence—whose clinching argument, though, must have been, 'I believe we will do more work in one day here than five down in Calcutta.' In 1864, the number of people who did that temporary migration from Calcutta to Simla was 484, including secretariat staff, clerks and servants. Needless to say, this number increased exponentially and by the turn of the century had risen at least four-fold.

Despite this, it still took a few more years for a formal announcement to be made; nonetheless, *ipso facto*, the Viceroy and his office spent the summers in Simla and this was the impetus for the town to grow ever larger. But over the course of time civic amenities had been enhanced, especially with regard to water and roads, both within the town and from outside for the transport of provisions. The long journey from Calcutta, which barely three decades ago involved a long and weary journey on the backs of horses and mules or

in carriages, as part of a caravan procession that could extend for miles, was now done by railway for the most part, reducing the time to a matter of days.

But from the very beginning, the British were quite clear that Simla was *their* town, a playground created by them and just for them, free of the encumbrance of the native populations they were forced to encounter in existing Indian cities. Here they could imagine that they were actually in Britain; they built the Gaiety Theatre to recreate the plays being shown in London and enjoyed the natural beauty of the outdoors in Annandale where they had fetes, played polo and cricket and had lively picnics. Social life was hectic; dinner parties and formal balls filled the calendar, and the earlier years of the Raj in Simla were replete with tales of the amorous indiscretions that caused gossip to spread like wildfire and were gleefully satirized in prose and verse by writers like Rudyard Kipling. Of course, that changed as Simla acquired officialdom, when the British penchant for hierarchy and precedence became increasingly evident and so much revolved around the Viceroy ensconced in the grey palace that was the Viceregal Lodge. One of its most lustrous occupants was Lord Curzon, the youngest Viceroy of India

The Gaiety Heritage Cultural Complex in Simla, on The Ridge

Nina with her cousin Anjali (known as Rosie) having tea at the Green Room at the Gaiety Theatre in Simla

in history, an unabashed Imperialist, yet one who declared: 'The East is a university in which the scholar never takes his degree'. He loved the pomp and ceremony of India, its colour and spectacle, and is remembered equally for his restoration of the Taj Mahal in Agra and his disastrous attempt to partition Bengal. He disliked inefficiency, delays and over-long notings on file; once, a draft was sent to him that was late in its submission, for which the official concerned apologized. Curzon's crisp response was: 'The delay is bad, but the draft is worse.' On another occasion, after going through a series of lengthy notes, he wrote: 'I agree with the gentleman whose signature looks like a trombone.'

Perhaps the only Indians who were accepted (even if not always on par) were the Princes of Indian states. They stood at the very apex of the Indian social scale, they were almost all wealthy and had lavish lifestyles, many of them were well-travelled and some well-educated. They were the natural leaders of their people, they were safe companions as long as they operated under the benign gaze of Empire, they had large land holdings, and it was

The Viceregal Lodge, Simla.

better to maintain good relations with them, a policy that had averted many potential crises during 1857. On occasion, their armies had augmented those of the British in a number of skirmishes. In earlier days, they were encouraged to come for the 'season'. Many of them came from the Punjab and bought properties: Nahan, Jind, Patiala, for example; later, there were families from much farther away and some of them acquired more than one property.

In the late 19th century, much to the alarm of the British, it was discovered that almost one-seventh of the property stock of large houses in Simla belonged to Indian princely families, and consequently the rules for purchase and sale were tightened. The Nizam of Hyderabad was not allowed to buy the Snowdon complex and Maharani Suniti Devi of Cooch Behar, who owned four properties, was made to sell off some part of her estate. In her autobiography, she observed: 'I do not know for what reason Lord Curzon, when Viceroy, insisted on my husband selling this property.' In a further turn of the screw, the Maharaja of Cooch Behar was denied permission to sell property to the Raja of Kapurthala, though sales to British buyers were encouraged. Now the rules became even more forbidding. Broad hints were issued that the Princes should not 'hang about' in the town. Furthermore, a formal visit required the permission of the Government of India, given only after due consideration of the purpose of the visit, the length of the stay and the place of residence. In 1904, two rulers, those of Dholpur and Cooch Behar, were not granted permission to visit Simla on the grounds that 'both have now spent more than they can afford.'

Coincidentally, it was in that very same year, 1904, that Nina's father-in-law, Raja Charanjit Singh, acquired Chadwick, the first house he bought in Simla and the home to which Kanwar Ripjit Singh brought his bride in 1935. Chadwick had been built in the late 19th century by General Marshall who had been Chief Engineer, Punjab, and later sold to Bishop Mathews, from whom he bought it. At the time he bought the property he was only in his early twenties, and we may speculate that this was the Raja's first truly independent home, his father, Kanwar Suchet Singh having passed away in 1901. He enlarged the property, and lavished care and attention upon it, doubtless sizable sums of money too, to make it one of the finest residences in Simla and worthy of respect for its taste and aesthetics. Much work went into its well-kept garden whose terraces were designed by a landscape gardener who had spent many years in Versailles. A particularly fine weeping willow tree with an interesting history stood on the premises; it was grown from a cutting of a tree which had been planted over the first grave of the Emperor Napoleon in St Helena by his medical attendant, a Dr O'Meara. He sent cuttings of this tree to his nephew in Simla, a Mr O'Meara who for many years was the only dental surgeon in Punjab, and the trees grew in a number of areas in and about the town, including the Raja's garden.

What was special about Chadwick, apart from the elegant house, was its location at the end of a spur. An admirer wrote:

> 'On three sides you look through space to the mountains, some nearer, some farther, and on the fourth side are trees and more trees effectively screening other habitations and making one feel a rest and quiet that never comes to the person whose every movement almost is overlooked by neighbouring windows.'

The views were charming and the Vicereine, Lady Chelmsford, painted some of her pictures from the lawns in the garden during their tenure from 1916 to 1921.

For whom had he created such a beautiful home? By then he was married and had two children, his older sons, Ajit and Sarabjit, who would have been very little boys when he bought Chadwick. Perhaps, in this essentially British milieu, he was preparing them for their eventual education in England as they played amidst apple trees and flower beds. We do not know if they ever attended school in Simla; it is very likely that as they grew up they were taught at home (as their youngest brother was), under the tutelage of a master who would see to the basics of a curriculum that almost certainly included the English language and how to speak it fluently.

Did he love them with a paternal warmth? We do not know, but in the context of the times we need to re-look at the definitions of 'love' and 'paternal'. In the Victorian era, aristocratic and upper-class children were tended to by nannies, governesses and tutors. In the British system they were meant to be seen occasionally but never heard. In the royal families of Punjab they often grew up together but with a keen and territorial awareness of hierarchy and inheritance. From his childhood, Raja Charanjit Singh must have heard a lot about the ferocious litigation between his uncle Raja Randhir Singh of Kapurthala and his father Kanwar Suchet Singh. The issue was the disputed will of their father, Raja Nihal Singh, who had sought to parcel out the state between his three sons, the largest part going to Randhir Singh and the remainder, with an income of Rs 2,00,000, equally divided between the other two. Despite the clarity of the will it was a long and bitter legal battle. At stake was the physical extent of the state of Kapurthala, and it was not in British interests to see the will fully complied with, as it would diminish the size and riches of an ally in a strategically located area. Eventually the matter was settled by the intervention of the Secretary of State, who granted an annual cash allowance for the two younger brothers, but ensured that the unaltered state remained with Raja Randhir Singh and his heirs and successors.

This decision of the British paid off handsomely in 1857 and 1858 when the Raja's troops defended or guarded Jullunder and Hoshiarpur against Indian freedom fighters in the Punjab; then went further afield to Awadh, where, it is recorded, he personally led his army in six engagements and captured several guns. For this he was richly rewarded by the grant of lucrative estates in Awadh which ensured him a very handsome income. And his status was much enhanced by being given precedence over all the great *taluqdars* of Awadh, the aristocratic landowners, and awarded the title of *Raja-i-Rajgan*. A few years later he was invested with the insignia of the Most Exalted Order of the Star of India at a special investiture, the first Punjab Prince to receive this honour. But he did not live very long to enjoy the fruits of his loyalty—he died in a ship en route to England before he was 40 years of age.

All this was well in the past by the mid-1930s, the time Nina came to Chadwick. At this point Raja Charanjit Singh had owned Chadwick for over three decades and his life followed a well-ordered annual cycle: his time was spent in Simla during the summer and Delhi for part of the winter. In both places, there were official functions that he had to fulfill as a Nominated Member of the Council of State. Then, Lucknow, even if for a brief time. Apart from catching up with old friends amongst the *taluqdars* of Awadh, there was now the added possibility of meeting his daughter, Pamela at her future home in Shahjahanpur in United Provinces (present day Uttar Pradesh) and perhaps a quick trip to his large landholding in Lionelpur which was not too far away and which later became Rajanagar to the family.

Life at Chadwick

Raja Charanjit Singh was as Anglophile as his kinsman, the ruler of Kapurthala, Maharaja Jagatjit Singh, was Francophile. The latter had built his palace in the style of Versailles, a magnificent edifice that took seven years to build. Its interiors were lavish, with Sevres ornaments, lapis lazuli pillars and Aubusson carpets. He also built a hunting lodge named Villa Buona Vista. Equally, in true secular spirit, he built noteworthy places of worship for his people including a mosque for his Muslim majority population, whose design replicated the grand Koutoubia Mosque of Marrakesh.

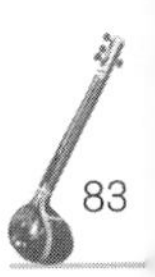

In correct Anglophile manner, in Simla, as elsewhere, each single day for Charanjit Singh was as meticulously organized as his year. Mealtimes were fixed and timings adhered to with strictness, except when he entertained, which he did with great frequency and lavishness. The Raja was known for his fine table, reputedly the one of the best in the whole of the Punjab. His staff maintained a register which scrupulously recorded the details of menus for previous lunches and dinners: the dates, the guests, the courses, the accompanying wines and their vintages, so that a menu was never repeated for a returning guest. The food served was the kind of Anglo-European cuisine found in the highest echelons of Simla society and it was pegged to achieve a consistent standard of excellence; anything less would not do for him. The meals would include soup and a variety of hors d'oeuvres, as well as delicacies such as salmon and lobster; mousses and dishes in aspic; game birds and pies followed by an Indian course and then trifles or eclairs or meringues as light as air.

Nina was plunged into this world almost from the time that she arrived; for her, it was a completely new experience and a daunting one. The kind of hospitality she was used to offering in her parents' house was also refined but its expression was completely different. No alcohol was ever served, but laid out on platters would be exquisitely cooked Bengali food, little cutlets of banana flowers or tender prawns in coconut cream. Here, to begin with, there was a bewildering and unfamiliar array of silverware and glassware to be set alongside the gleaming china on the table. She could not bring herself to ask the smartly liveried serving staff how it was done; instead, she tip-toed behind the butlers to see how they laid the table, and her instinctive eye and feeling for style picked up the differences in the shapes and sizes of the glassware and flatware and the hidden rhythms of their usage. As seating by precedence at the table was a strictly-observed rule, and the guest list could well include the viceroy or the commander-in-chief or similar august personages, another complicated aspect was the correct placing of name cards. It was a far cry from the warm informal gatherings that characterized the social circles of her parents: the ease of knowing people as long-term family friends or through shared interests, such as literature or music.

The finer points of etiquette, all the formalities of being an official hostess and the art of polite conversation had to be mastered; but her quickness, her facility for instantly absorbing and learning—these came to her rescue. They were qualities that stayed with her all her life and served her well on more than one occasion.

Her intuition told her that her father-in-law expected nothing less than the best from her, and she understood that, for in her own way she, too, was a perfectionist. And so she undertook tasks that she need not have done herself—arranging flowers, for example, vase after vase in multiples, partly because she enjoyed doing so and partly because she knew that she could make the presentation more impeccable by adding her own natural aesthetic sense. Her development as the chatelaine of the Raja's household was swift and more than satisfactory, but whether he communicated his approval is not known. Unlikely, since he probably took for granted that his life and his home would proceed along the strict and disciplinary lines that he had laid down so long ago, into which everyone around him would simply fall into place.

Luckily, there was Pamela, young and on the verge of becoming a bride herself, with whom she developed a close friendship in the few months left to her in Simla. Nina had come west, now Pamela was going east; perhaps they compared notes and laughed a little over their dissimilar fates. She was marrying into the respected and distinguished Prasada family, who had been zamindars in Shahjahanpur and its environs for more than a century. Her future father-in-law, Kanwar Jwala Prasada, was a member of the Imperial Civil Service (forerunner of the ICS) and served as Deputy Commissioner of Hardoi; and her mother-in-law was a Tagore, Purnima Devi, the daughter of Hemendranath Tagore. In the strange way that multiple threads tie people's histories together, she was the grand-daughter of Debendranath Tagore, the same Tagore who had long ago sheltered Keshub Chandra Sen, Nina's grandfather, when he became a member of the Brahmo Samaj, and from whom he had parted when the Brahmo Samaj split in the schism of 1866. But that was in the past and the wounds had healed; long ago, in 1910,

Debendranath's son, Rabindranath Tagore, had dissolved any bitterness by acknowledging Keshub Sen's universalism and his complete understanding of the unity underlying religious diversity. In a public address he said: 'When I realized this, all my earlier antagonism for him vanished and I came to pay him homage.'

Rip's sister Pamela, on her wedding day, with bridegroom Jyoti Prasada

Purnima Devi was, as most of the Tagore women were, a lady of many accomplishments. She spoke several languages, including Sanskrit, Hindi, Urdu and French, played the violin and the piano, was a seasoned big game hunter along with her husband, and an expert horsewoman who rode around their extensive lands. She was keenly interested in the education of women, and set up a school for girls; she also set up a number of Purdah Clubs with a view to improving the lot of ladies who were allowed no public voice. For her many social reform movements, she had been awarded the *Kaiser-i-Hind* medal in 1910.

The parents-in-law of Rip's sister, Pamela; eminent zamindar Jwala Prasada and Poornima Prasada, formerly Sudakshana Tagore

It was a situation made for sharing between the two young women and made their bonds stronger. Just as Pamela taught Nina much that she needed to know about Simla and Chadwick, Nina told Pamela all that she knew about the Tagore family.

But in all her endeavours, it was her husband who helped her most in dealing with the newness of her situation and coping with the demands of his father. Kanwar Ripjit Singh, or Rip, was a tall, good-looking man who was warm and affectionate despite (or maybe because of) his father's distant nature. He loved the outdoor life, doted on his wife and guided her through the social thickets of life and friendship she was about to encounter in a variety of places: Simla, very formal and very anglicized; Lucknow and Awadh, where a rooted high culture permeated the land like a fragrance that wafted over everyday life, language, garments, food, music, art; and the farm at Lionelpur, which was to become their own special idyll.

But there was one area where he could not help her and where she remained inconsolable. Gone were those carefree, music-filled days of Lily Cottage. Here in her husband's home, singing was not considered a suitable art for a lady of good family; it was the domain of prostitutes and kept women. So embedded was this taboo that she was not allowed to sing in Chadwick. Elsewhere, it was restricted to the confines of the women's area and only for an audience of women. Her music practice was conducted secretly; it was possible only in the deepest recesses of their private apartments.

Kanwar Ripjit Singh

Children and Chapslee

Much as she missed her music, life was busy for Nina. Moving between homes in different cities was a time-consuming process; now, to add to that, she also had two very young daughters to look after, Nilika and Rena, or June and Billy as they were known, and the prospect of a new home in Simla.

As beautiful and gracious as Chadwick was, it was situated in the suburbs of Simla, a good distance away from the centre of town. Possibly Raja Charanjit Singh thought it was time to look around for a suitable home with better access to the needs of a growing family. By a stroke of luck, just such a house now appeared on the market. One day, Rip and Nina were having tea with his father at the famous restaurant, Davicos, on a fashionable stretch of the Mall. As Rip took a stroll down the Mall, he met a property agent who told him, 'You were enquiring about Chapslee not long ago. Well, it's on the market now, it's available if you wish to buy it.' Chapslee was one of the oldest houses of Simla. It had a pedigree of distinguished owners, and was once described as 'eminently suitable for the summer residence of a Ruling Chief.'

Within days, before the end of October 1938, the deal was closed and the large double-storied house passed into the hands of the Singh family. But the ever-meticulous Charanjit Singh needed to pull it into shape before moving in, so the whole of the following year was spent in essential modifications: the installation of electricity, lights and modern bathrooms, the stylish re-papering and re-furbishing of the interiors, and the addition of elegance to its décor. As a historian of Simla describes it,

> The panelling, false ceiling and staircases are teak with wood-parquet on the floors. Murano chandeliers, maroon velvet curtains from the Doge's Palace in Venice, Gobelin and Flemish tapestries, displays of arms and hunting trophies, and Delft-tiled fireplaces – complete with bellows and adirons – exquisite rugs and a fine collection of furniture still evoke the heyday of the burra sahib.

But Chapslee was more than just a beautiful building. On its elegant shoulders it carried the full weight of history and the first rumblings of the Great Game between Britain and Russia, which was played out in the battle grounds of Afghanistan. The original owner, a Dr Blake, divided his plot of land into two, one for a larger house which he intended to let out and a smaller one for his own residence. In 1836, he sold the larger property to Lord Auckland, then the Governor General, and the smaller one to his nephew, Capt. the

Hon'ble W. G. Osbourne who was also his Military Secretary. The larger house immediately became Auckland House and later Government House, while its smaller adjunct was called Secretary's Lodge (later Chapslee) as it housed the offices of the military and private secretaries and became a space for important meetings.

It was from a meeting room in Chapslee that the famous (or infamous, depending on your point of view) Simla Manifesto was declared on 1st October 1838 which effectively launched the First Anglo-Afghan War, a disaster that was later dubbed Auckland's Folly. It was a wheels-within-wheels maze of conflicting and colluding interests which included the British, the powerful Sikh Empire of Maharaja Ranjit Singh, the faction-ridden Afghans, the Russians and the Qajar dynasty of Persia. It was a show of power that brought together the two greatest armies of the subcontinent, the French-trained and well-equipped Dal Khalsa of the Sikhs and the British and Sepoy troops of the East India Company. The alleged reason was the restoration of the Afghan throne to the former Emir Shah Shuja as opposed to the pro-Russian Emir Dost Mohammed. This 'Grand Army of the Indus' achieved its objective in Kabul within the year, but soon tasted defeat at the hands of rebel Afghans. The eventual outcome was a stunning defeat for Britain and the futile massacre of its citizens and of military and Sikh forces as they scrambled through gorges and across snow-bound mountain passes in humiliating retreat. A British chaplain summed it up with this mournful epitaph: 'Not one benefit, political or military, was acquired with this war. Our eventual evacuation of the country resembled the retreat of an army defeated.'

Such a drastic failure of policy had to be acknowledged. And so, from the very same room in Chapslee, and on the very same day exactly four years later in 1842, Auckland's successor, Lord Ellenborough, announced that the Government's intentions had changed and a new foreign policy would come into effect to restore and maintain peace in Asia. Surely a statement of grim humour, for barely a month before, British forces had entered Kabul and burnt down its great bazaar as a symbol of their revenge.

Chapslee on Elysium Hill, a lovingly preserved heritage home

In the five-odd decades that followed, the house went through several owners until in 1896 it was bought by an eminent citizen of Simla, Sir Arthur Milford Ker. He was by profession a banker; he was an erudite personality who possessed an extensive library and was a great friend of Lord Curzon. It was he who altered subtly the alignment of Chapslee, retaining part of the old structure but building all around it, keeping the original intact. He changed the direction of the house from south-facing to west-facing by adding a porch, making it more comfortable for its inhabitants. After the deaths of Sir Arthur and his widow, the property was left to a nephew who lived in England, and it was from him that it was bought by the Raja.

Nina and her family moved into Chapslee in the summer of 1940, two weeks before her first son and third child, Ratanjit, was born. It became the house where her children grew up when they were in Simla for the hot summer months of their holidays; and the home from where their most vivid memories of their grandfather, whom they called Papaji, came. For all four (including Karanjit, Nina and Ripjit's second son and youngest child) he was a major influence in their lives in the traditions and behaviours that they absorbed from him: he was like an exemplar that they had to follow, a strict disciplinarian and autocrat who believed that children should be seen but never heard. Conversation was limited as they could speak only when they were spoken to. The indulgent love of a grandparent was singularly missing, and as they grew up, Nina explained the lack of love in Charanjit Singh's own childhood as a reason for his stern hardness, an alienation that made him cold. The warmth of a hug was never his to give, nor, sadly, to receive; a cursory pat on a child's head was as much as could expected. Karanjit, a clear favourite from infancy, was probably the first baby he ever picked up, and as Nina handed him to his grandfather he wet his nappy and was nearly dropped.

Life in Chapslee was regimented, pretty much like Charanjit Singh's own life. As little children the girls were looked after by nannies, who would see to their morning grooming and washing, after which they were taken to meet their parents, who were sleepily enjoying their first cups of tea, then to

LEFT Nina's three older children: (L to R) Rena, Ratanjit and Nilika (Billy, Reggie and June)
RIGHT Little Karanjit (Kenny) in Mummy's arms

breakfast in the children's dining room. In the late morning, they would be taken to meet their grandfather and they were trained to bow respectfully low and fold their hands as they greeted him. Any kind of noisiness or boisterousness befitting their age was strongly discouraged; they had to be very quiet and tip-toe around the house in order not to disturb Papaji. The lawn was a favourite place, because here they could sing nursery rhymes and play little games, though presumably they were not allowed to shriek or roll in the grass or engage in any form of the spontaneity so natural to children. Their days were mapped out, ending in early suppers and early bed, lulled to sleep by the stories read out by the nannies and a goodnight kiss from the parents.

As they grew older and the nannies were replaced by school, they were groomed in table manners: how to eat, what not to do, and they learnt the proper etiquette for forks and knives, which ones to use and when. It was a rule that nothing could be left on the plate; there was no question of preferences in food or refusing to eat this or that. Side by side there were lessons in the more formal etiquette of Simla society, which would serve them equally in Delhi or Lucknow; how to courtesy, for example, to wish the viceroy or other British notables, or how to greet Indian royalty and the great landowners of Awadh gracefully with a low bow and folded hands.

But surely the most exciting time for the young girls was hanging from the balustrade of the upstairs gallery in Simla to see the fascinating galaxy of dinner guests thronging the halls of Chapslee. They would look to see who was arriving and marvel at the dresses of the ladies; they would inhale the intoxicating whiffs of perfume trailed by women en route to the cloakroom to hang up their outer clothes; and later the fragrant smoke of cigars wafting up as the men relaxed in the smoking room. From that gallery they could see people like Auchinleck, the Commander-in-Chief, who once came with his sister; and many other such notables at whom they gazed in wonder with the fervent hope that they themselves would not be seen. As a little boy,

The sun room, light and airy, filled with potted plants and flowers

Ratanjit would be dressed like a miniature raja, complete with an ornamented turban, and placed upon a chair by his father to garland honoured guests like the Vicereine, Lady Linlithgow, as she arrived for lunch.

The tranquil garden at Chapslee

Rajanagar and Delhi

Chapslee was all formality and the real relaxation for Nina, Ripjit and the children only came when they visited their farm in Lionelpur situated between Sitapur and Shahjahanpur on the national highway from Lucknow. The vast tract of land had belonged to the family for close to a century, bought by Suchet Singh in the mid-19th century, and the croplands were supervised by a local munshi or manager. Now it made sense to build a house there: they were surrounded by the lands of their friends; Ripjit's sister Pamela was not too far away in Shahjahanpur; and most importantly, just a few years ago Ripjit had taken over as the administrator of the large estate and its staff and needed a place for himself and his family.

It was Nina who drew the rough sketch for the plan of the house they would build. She was not an architect, but she was guided by a very clear idea of what she wanted and by her unerring aesthetic instinct. Her vision for the exteriors and elegant interior spaces favoured the bold modernist

The dining room with beautifully crafted chiffoniers and vitrines

The elegant drawing room with Gobelin tapestries and portraiture

The hall at Chapslee with a spectacular clerestory and a handsome wooden staircase

EXTREME LEFT The well-appointed dining room

LEFT Detail of the staircase at Chapslee

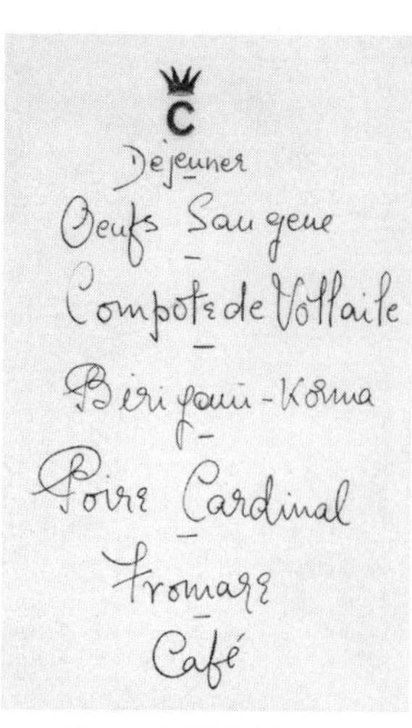
C
Dejeuner
Oeufs Sau gene
—
Compote de Vollaile
—
Beriyani - Korma
—
Poire Cardinal
—
Fromage
—
Café

Menu for the Vicereine's lunch, handwritten by Nina

RIGHT A splendidly attired Reggie waits to garland the Vicereine

BELOW Chapslee plays host to the Vicereine (seated centre)

LEFT Strolling in the grounds with Nina, Raja Sahib in his plus fours and Homburg hat
RIGHT Tikka Raja Paramjit Singh of Kapurthala (extreme right) with his entourage

lines, the fine craftsmanship and the sophistication of the Art Deco style, which was very much in vogue at that time. While the house was being constructed they lived in a makeshift set of rooms in Kotra, a tiny nearby village, braving the inclement weather and swarms of mosquitos, so that Ripjit could supervise the building and consult Nina when needed. And finally, by 1940, the house was ready: it was a very compact yet luxurious house with well-appointed spacious rooms and large en-suite dressing rooms. There was a beautiful marble fireplace in the living room, high like the ones in Chapslee but without the over-mantles, and the building was set like a jewel surrounded by beautiful gardens. Both husband and wife were delighted and promptly named it Raja Kothi, and that is how the farm was called Rajanagar.

For Ripjit Singh, it was a very special place, it was his home with Nina. 'Our idyll, Nina,' he would tell her, 'this is our rural idyll'.

The house at Rajanagar, Rip and Nina's rural idyll

Ripjit Singh, or Rip as he was called, was a tall, big man: a large human being filled with warmth and affection. He was a dapper, well-dressed gentleman fond of clothes and ties. Indeed, he had an obsession about ties, he would match his suits to his ties rather than the other way round. When Charanjit Singh watched him as a small child, no doubt he was reminded of his two older sons, how he had sent them away for their education and how subsequently an irreparable rift had occurred. He did not wish to lose this son; better, then, to keep him by his side and have him tutored at home. So he appointed a Colonel William Andrews, a man well known in the field of education, to teach him at home and years after the process was over, Rip took over Rajanagar (then called Lionelpur) and began to supervise the work of the farm on visits from Lucknow. During this time, Rip must have realized how much his father feared losing him and recognized the love that was hidden beneath the surface coldness. So also did Nina: even through the most terrible of times, she kept telling her children: 'Remember how much your father loved him. Always remember that, no matter what you think or what you hear of your grandfather...'

Rip liked the good things of life. He was an avid huntsman and had a choice collection of guns, which he used for bird hunting, bagging green pigeon, partridge and quail for the cookpot much to his children's delight. While his father was a connoisseur of fine wines, he had a select collection of Scotch whisky which he loved. He also had a collection of cars, another of his passions and one that both his sons inherited. His garage included a Daimler, a Mercedes 500 Tourer with an open hood, and a Packard.

Kanwar Ripjit Singh resplendent in his feathered *sarpech*, bears the CIE medal on his chest

If Chapslee was Raja Charanjit Singh, Rajanagar was entirely Ripjit Singh; for his children it remained forever the happiest memory of their childhood, because they were all together and had their parents all to themselves. It was a large sugarcane farm, and one of the first things Rip taught his children was how to strip off the outer skin of the cane with their teeth and chew on the sweet fibrous flesh inside. But more than that, Rajanagar was freedom, a place where they could run around barefoot, unfettered by formality, or walk through seemingly unending fields of cane and mustard or splash across inundated paddy fields. They would drive to the surrounding wetlands to see the little ducks and the fish. Their modes of transport were endless—a bullock cart on country lanes, a tractor across fields, and best of all, a huge Bedford truck where an open back was spread out with sofas and chairs for all of them to sit on as they went singing and laughing to visit a nearby friend or simply for a drive. It was a new concept of space and freedom: running carefree to the faint line that marked the horizon, sliding down haystacks, trotting on ponies, enveloped in the warmth and affection of their parents.

Rip delighted in making his children happy. During the winter festival of Lohri stacks of cane would be piled up for a bonfire; when lit, the wood crackled and exploded like a bomb going off and they would all clap their hands with glee.

Rip's open-hearted and welcoming hospitality made Rajanagar a watering hole for all the nearby zamindars from Powayan, Pilibhit, Bijwa and Katiyari. Friends and family arrived from Sitapur, Pamela and her family from Shahjahanpur. His huge parties were legendary; when the main house ran out of rooms for guests, swiss cottages or tents were put up on the spacious lawns complete with bedrooms and dressing rooms to accommodate the overflow.

He loved cooking; that was an essential part of his hospitality. His preference was for the spiced yet subtle Mughlai dishes or the rich cuisine of Rampur. There were always visitors, always parties, especially cooking parties with Rip centre stage presiding in the open air over a procession of assistants who lit the cook fires and braziers, brought out the vessels, ingredients and ground spices, and faithfully followed his directions. At some point the hookahs

The wide open spaces of the Rajanagar farm, a playground for the children

The jheels were filled with duck and other waterbirds

would emerge, smoky and fragrant with flowers, to engage the expectant adult audience of friends sitting around; there was an even larger number of expectant children hovering about wondering what was being cooked, and hoping it might be green pigeons from the morning's shoot.

Of course, Charanjit Singh was also present. But here, it was different. He had his side of the house and Ripjit and his family had theirs, allowing the children the freedom to run around in that vast space of the farm; there were no restrictions as there were in Chapslee. Here they could do whatever they liked and the times spent at Rajanagar were blissful for them.

Delhi, city of Durbars

In Delhi things were different again. In the latter half of the 1930s and into the 1940s it was still early days for this newly-created capital city, whose unmistakable purpose was to represent the ruling power of the Raj. Its very location, placing the Viceroy's House at commanding heights atop Raisina Hill overlooking the offices of the Government of India and the broad sweep of King's Way, carried a message of invincibility. It seemed to flow seamlessly from memories of the grand durbars that had been held in the northern area of the old city to mark the succession of British monarchs in the aptly-named Coronation Park.

The children could romp around with their pets at Rajanagar

Diwali celebrations at Rajanagar as hundreds of diyas light up the house

Group photograph: (L to R) Jyoti Prasada, Nina, Sir Maurice Hallett, Governor of U.P., Raja Charanjit Singh, Pamela and Rip. Seated on the ground, Nina's daughters June (left) and Billy (right) flank their two cousins Jai and Jity with brother Reggie in the centre

INSET Baby June and Pamela's son Jity, both first-borns, seen together in this picture

Winter 1948, Rip's last get-together with his friends, the zamindars of Awadh from Nanpura, Powayan and Katiyari

The use of the word 'durbar', a term steeped with meaning in the context of Indian royal families and therefore familiar to Indians, was deliberate. It now placed the role of over-arching ruler, the paramount power, in the hands of the British. And it did so in a spectacular manner and on vast scale (the Viceroy, Lord Lytton, was of the opinion that Indians loved 'a bit of bunting'). The first durbar, held in 1877 in honour of the reigning monarch, Queen Victoria, was called the Proclamation Durbar for here it was that the Queen was first proclaimed the Empress of India. And here also her Proclamation of 1858—following the first Indian uprising for independence in 1857—was read out 19 years later by Lord Lytton:

> Now...we do by these presents notify and declare that...we have taken upon ourselves the...government (of the territories of India) and we hereby call upon all our subjects within the said territories to be faithful and to bear true allegiance to us, our heirs and successors, and to submit themselves to the authority of those whom we may hereafter, from time to time, see fit to appoint to administer the government of our said territories, in our name and on our behalf...

The Viceroy's House, renamed as Rashtrapati Bhavan on 26 January 1950

In this smooth and silken manner the conquest, which had begun innocuously enough with the purchase of three villages by the banks of the Hooghly River some two centuries ago, came full circle through phases of history to blanket a whole country. And India had passed as an Imperial possession from the hands of the British East India Company into those of the British Crown. The Durbar of 1877, with its message of clemency from Empress Victoria, was intended perhaps to look forward to a peaceful and productive future and close the tense chapter of the events of 1857; equally, to allow the British to occupy the now vacant Mughal throne in the full gaze of all the Indian princes gathered there.

The next Coronation Durbar was held in 1903 by Lord Curzon, an unabashed lover of pomp and spectacle; this event was to mark the succession of Edward VII and Alexandra as Emperor and Empress of India. To his immense disappointment, the monarch could not attend, sending instead his brother the Duke of Connaught. But that did not stop Curzon from planning a fortnight of unmatched pageantry and festivities: a grand processional entry, receptions and lavish banquets, sporting events like polo, military reviews, exhibitions of Indian art, massed bands and a Coronation Ball. The backdrop for these happenings was an entire tented city created within the space of months with residences and well-tended gardens, complete with modern installations for electricity and sanitation, civic amenities such as a Post Office (with its own stamps), a hospital and police force, even a temporary light railway to transport the admiring crowds he knew would flock from Delhi.

Yet, all intentions apart, the expenditure and effort came in for criticism from sections of the Indian press and the newly-formed Indian National Congress. Both durbars came at the time of famine years. It seemed inhuman to waste money on spectacle and feasting when so many had died of hunger and thousands were still in relief camps. Some bitterly dubbed this the 'Curzonation Durbar': one paper said it was 'an extravagant waste'; another called the exhibition 'a glorified bazaar'.

By the time the third Durbar of 1911 came around, things had changed. To begin with, this durbar was to be graced by the presence of the King Emperor

and Empress, George V and Mary, the first ruling monarchs to visit India and surely that put a different perspective on things. Yes, it did. It heightened the scale and led to some surprises. In 1877, the number of Indian princes attending the durbar was recorded as 63, which went up to 100 in 1903. The protocols remained the same in 1911: in a large shamiana surrounded by a huge amphitheatre of distinguished guests, British officials and Indian princes paid homage to the Crown and George V and Mary were introduced to over one hundred maharajas and ruling princes.

Once again, magic was created. Within the 'wilderness' of the Red Fort, fountains and water runnels sprang to life; lawns, shrubberies and stately pavilions appeared; and seating to accommodate 100,000 people and space for 30,000 troops were carved out. An open space of approximately 80 sq miles was transformed into a tented city complete with gardens; the King-Emperor's camp alone covered an area of some 85 acres. During the Durbar, the monarch and his wife appeared in their Coronation robes and full regalia on the balcony of the Red Fort to reveal themselves to the people in a sort of a darshan; 'about 100,000 people' thronged to see their ruler at this public audience.

The Delhi Durbar in 1911 of King George V and Queen Mary

The Nizam of Hyderabad, Osman Ali Khan, Asif Jah VII, pays homage to King George V and Queen Mary at the Delhi Durbar, 1911

It was during this Durbar that the King-Emperor announced two decisions: one, to shift the capital from Calcutta to Delhi, a move that had been contemplated from several viewpoints. Firstly, Calcutta was to the extreme east and its position there as capital was 'long ... recognised to be a serious anomaly'. A more central location would be practical in many ways and Delhi seemed an obvious choice. It had age-old connections as a capital city; it had acquired legendary status as a seat of power for a number of dynasties through the course of history. It aroused the enthusiasm of the British. The Viceroy, Lord Hardinge, had written: 'Delhi is still a name to conjure with...' which the Secretary of State for India, the Marquess of Crewe, had supported in another letter: '... these ancient walls of Delhi enshrine an Imperial tradition comparable with that of Constantinople, or with that of Rome itself...' In addition, Bengal had long been the scene of growing opposition to British rule in India, especially since the province had been partitioned in 1905. There was a call for the boycott of British goods, and violence erupted by way of bombings and assassinations. The political climate was becoming more hostile, so the second decision announced by the monarch, namely, the revoking of the Bengal partition, was an attempt to at least partially rectify that. But given the circumstances no further persuasion for the move to Delhi was needed.

The new capital city of Delhi was completed in 1931, somewhat delayed because of the intervention of World War I. From the very beginning it was meant to be a symbol of Empire, an Imperial capital with imperial architecture. But it had to be sited far away enough from Mughal Delhi, from the city that the Emperor Shah Jahan had built, so that nostalgic

memories of an older empire were not aroused. With this in mind, an area to the south of the city was selected where there was space for the city to grow beyond its borders when required. The two architects who worked on the design and construction, Edwin Lutyens and Herbert Baker, were keenly aware of what was expected of them, and Baker articulated it thus: 'British rule in India...is a new civilisation in growth, a blend of the best elements of East and West...It is to this great fact that the architecture of Delhi should bear testimony.'

Another concept was embedded in the layout of the city, namely, locations arranged in hierarchies. The Viceroy's House was the most important building; perched on top of Raisina Hill, it became the centre-point around which clustered those other buildings and residences that reduced in importance the further away they were. Ruling princes, like Baroda, Jaipur and Hyderabad, were allocated large spaces for palatial residences grouped around the India Gate in a straight line from the foot of the Hill, as if perenially under the benign gaze of the Viceroy. Proximity to the centre, and the size of bungalows and compounds were markers of ranking, certain roads reflected greater prestige than others; this was almost like the order of precedence used for seating, except it was now played out on a scale much larger than a dining table.

For Raja Charanjit Singh, living in the new city of Delhi was a necessity due to his appointment as a Nominated Member of the Council of State. He was somewhat of a veteran in this post, having served four consecutive Councils of State, spanning a time frame from 1921 to approximately the mid-1940s.

The initiative for this institution had come from the Secretary of State for India, Lord Montagu, who served from 1917 to 1922. In his opinion, the Indian administration was 'too wooden, too iron, too inelastic, too antediluvian...' for modern purposes. These purposes were, in short, the greater involvement of Indians in the affairs of their own country. His plea, made in a famous address in the British Parliament in 1917, was for the 'increasing association of Indians in every branch of the administration and the gradual development of self-governing institutions ... (for) responsible government in India as part of the British Empire.' This paved the way for the proposed Montagu-Chelmsford Reforms (Lord Chelmsford being then the Viceroy of India) which became an Act in 1919 and led to the formation of a bi-cameral federal legislature, the Indian Legislative Assembly and the Council of State, corresponding roughly to Lower and Upper Houses respectively; the former being largely elected and the latter partially nominated and partially elected by a restricted or chosen electorate.

The perceived role of the members of the Council of State was expressed by the Montford Report: 'In as much as the Council of State will be the supreme legislative authority for India...we desire to attract to it the services of the best men available in the country...the Council of State should develop something of the experience and dignity of a body of Elder Statesmen... (and) ensure that their status and position and record of services will give to the Council a senatorial character...' This body of 'Elder Statesmen' comprised 60 members, of which 27 were nominated and the rest elected on broad-based representation from all major provinces across the country and included Muslims and Sikhs.

Needless to say, this was not an entirely altruistic move by the British. From the beginning it was clear that this was a 'checks and balances' situation where the members of the Council of State had the power to veto and block anything sent up from the Legislative Assembly that was too alarmingly progressive, acting as 'a safety valve for Imperial interest'. But in all fairness, it should be noted that on occasion the Council also played mediator between the Assembly and the Government, seeking to reconcile points of view through negotiation and mutual accommodation. Some social reform measures, such as the Hindu Women's Right to Property Act of 1928, were passed, thanks to the intervention of the Council.

The meetings of the Council were held in Delhi at the historic Metcalfe House which meant that Charanjit Singh spent at least part of the winter in the city in his newly-acquired house on Akbar Road, a spacious bungalow

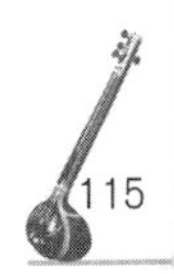

set in ample grounds, where Nina once again performed her duty as his official hostess in the formal drawing room decorated in rose-pink damask or the celadon-coloured dining room. The Simla standards were maintained: formal, exquisite, elegant with all the trappings of Chapslee. Membership of the Council meant access not only to the highest echelons of officialdom but also to a host of fellow members from across India, men who were leaders and thinkers and contributed significantly to its proceedings, such as Pheroze Sethna from Bombay and Sir C. Sankaran Nair from Madras (now Chennai). For all that the Raja was an Anglophile, he was also a scholar of Persian and presumably fluent in Urdu; he must then have delighted in conversations with the likes of Sir Ameeruddin Ahmad Khan of Loharu, or Raja Nawab Ali Khan from the United Provinces or Nawab Hayat Khan Noon of Punjab. Amongst the people he met, he would have already known some, such as his cousin, Raja Sir Harnam Singh, who had once been his neighbour on Summerhill, and was the father of Rajkumari Amrit Kaur, who became the first Health Minister of independent India.

Winter in New Delhi, even when the visit was limited to the length of Council meetings, also meant some participation in what was considered the height of the season, a time when the Viceroy had descended from Simla and was in residence. It was the Simla of the early 20th century all over again, the endless round of dinner parties, the garden parties, polo; there was also the New Delhi Horse Show Week whose grand climax was the Viceregal Ball. There were splendid investiture ceremonies held in the halls of the Viceroy's House, surely a palace to beat all palaces, where the pomp and ceremony of the Raj was displayed to the hilt. By the early 1940s, however, changing circumstances brought about alterations. There was a war going on, and a general air of sobriety was prevalent. Some glittering events—such as the Horse Show—were cancelled for the duration of the war. The Viceregal move to Simla was cut down to three weeks and the town now became the headquarters for the exiled Burmese government. The events on the eastern front convinced many people that there was a serious threat to Delhi; indeed, Raja Charanjit Singh was told that Delhi was sure to be bombed and it would be wise to move out of there. At this point, much else was changing on the national front; the Council of State had been expanded but its life span was uncertain, and a future in Delhi was a questionable proposition for the family, so the house was sold and the family looked to its other properties.

Awadh

And their gaze turned back to Awadh. Awadh, Rajanagar, Lucknow and the house at Outram Road: these were all places whose links were embedded in family history, which in some ways was entwined with the history of the state. Long decades ago, Suchet Singh (or Bade Sarkar as he was called), Rip's grandfather, had bought this property, before the events of 1857, before the exile of Nawab Wajid Ali Shah. He had been a great friend of the Nawab's brother, Sulaiman Qadr, a bond so close that they pledged loyalty to one another through an exchange of turbans, they broke bread together and called themselves brothers. As the turmoil of the 1857 uprising churned through Awadh, Bade Sarkar was one of the few who did not join the British forces, as did other princes, who were subsequently rewarded with huge and lucrative estates. Whatever land the Suchet Singh family had acquired in the rich doab area of the Gangetic plains was through purchase.

Awadh itself had a chequered history and from the 18th century onward had to face the growing avarice of the East India Company. It was a province of the Mughal Empire, but as the power of the Empire began to wane, its grip over its feudatories began to loosen. The founder of the dynasty of the Nawabs was Saadat Khan, a Persian from Nishapur, who was appointed the Governor of Awadh in 1722 and set up his capital in Faizabad, not far from Lucknow. It was the third Nawab, Shuja-ud-Daulah, who brought Faizabad to glory with the many beautiful buildings he bestowed on the city, including a fort and palaces. Unfortunately, neither he nor his city was destined to prosper for long.

In the fateful Battle of Buxar in 1764 the Nawab Shuja-ud-Daulah had sided with Mir Qasim, the fugitive Nawab of Bengal, no doubt seeking to ward off any future trouble from the British for himself. But Buxar was a rout:

Shuja-ud-Daulah was defeated in a very decisive manner and not only did he have to pay huge penalties, he had to turn over part of his territories to the British. It was the first nibble of the very large bites that the East India Company had in store for Awadh. His son and successor, Asaf-ud-Daula, shifted his capital to Lucknow, thereby dimming any future glory for Faizabad; he did, however, lay the foundation of what was to become a great city, one of unparalleled renown, whose name would be synonymous with superb architecture and a culture of astonishing elegance and refinement. It was said that he made the move because he wanted to escape from the clutches of a domineering mother. If that is really the case, then he had jumped straight from the frying pan into the fire, for the British appointed a Resident in Lucknow in 1773.

And that, you might say, was the beginning of the end.

A fifth Nawab followed, who was forced to abdicate because he had foolishly alienated not only his own people, but also the British, who then placed on the throne of Awadh the puppet king Saadat Ali Khan. In the Treaty of 1801, Saadat Ali Khan signed away his patrimony and the self-respect of his people. Half of the territory of Awadh was ceded to the British. His own troops had to be disbanded and replaced by British armed forces, an army of little use to him for which he was paying vast sums of money. Awadh was reduced to a vassal of the East India Company who now also had virtually unlimited access to its huge treasuries from which they drew 'loans' at ridiculous rates of 'interest'. In a way, history was repeating itself, Awadh was slipping out of the grasp of the Nawabs just as it had slipped out of the hands of the Mughals: but until the early years of the 19th century, the pretence of being a feudatory of the Mughals was maintained. An Awadh silver rupee struck in 1814 still carried the name of Emperor Shah Alam II; from 1819, coins no longer mentioned the Mughal emperor, but were struck in the Nawab's own name. Though increasingly, that meant nothing.

By this time, the state of Awadh was already a British Protectorate, as successive Nawabs, though nominally autonomous, came more and more under the jurisdiction of the Company. The nature of this relationship was to render the Nawabs ever weaker, their treasuries drained and their trade dislocated. They paid more attention to pomp and show and less to governance. As one writer stated, 'The sensuous life…did not reflect sheer perversity or weakness of character on the part of the Nawabs. Indolence was rather the only appropriate response to the situation in which the Princes of Oudh were placed…' Finally in 1856 the state was annexed under the Doctrine of Lapse, a policy devised by Lord Dalhousie, the Governor General for the East India Company, who had once famously said of Awadh that it was 'a cherry which will drop into our mouths some day. It has long been ripening'. According to the Doctrine, any state under the paramountcy of the Company would be automatically annexed if the ruler was either manifestly incompetent or died without a male heir. The question of who was incompetent was, of course, decided by the British, and in the incumbent, Nawab Wajid Ali Shah, they had a prime candidate. The Nawab was first imprisoned, then exiled to Calcutta where he died some 30 years later.

This set off the chain of events of 1857 that is now variously known as the Great Uprising, the First War of Independence or the Indian Mutiny, during which the control of Awadh was taken back by those who rebelled. Birjis Qadr, the young son of Wajid Ali Shah and Begum Hazrat Mahal, was placed on the throne in Lucknow, the famous Siege of Lucknow took place, and it took the British some months to re-take the area. And then the cherry finally and definitively fell into the waiting British mouth.

Nawab Wajid Ali Shah, an engraving from 1872

We may choose to view Nawab Wajid Ali Shah in many different ways: as the debauched ruler of British belief who spent his time not in the serious business of governance but in pursuits like singing and dancing and marrying

any woman who caught his fancy (including, once, a pretty water carrier), or as the melancholy ruler whom the British thwarted at every turn and whose kingdom they finally stole; or as the beloved figure whose subjects wept as he left his city for exile, mourning his departure with a beating of breasts and much lamentation. But in many ways it is he who brings together the myriad strands of the high culture that we think of as 'Lakhnavi'. As the Mughal Empire slipped into decline and court patronage became hard to come by, people of different skills chose to move from Delhi to Lucknow where the court had both taste and money: poets, musicians and dancers, painters and craftsmen, embroiderers and tailors. And it was in Lucknow that the palate of the gourmet came to a high point of refinement, as did the cult of the courtesan. Most significantly, it was the court of Awadh that nurtured the syncretic 'Ganga-Jamuni *tehzeeb*', the composite culture of 'gold and silver' that brought together Hindu and Muslim traditions.

Despite the great upheavals of historic events, the culture was sustained by the surviving aristocracy who were mostly from the great landowning families of the *taluqdars* and zamindars. They had traditionally played a very important role in the administration of Awadh though the powers of each of these two groups were flexible and differed somewhat. Nonetheless, both were able to live lives of leisure and affluence which enabled them to be patrons of the arts at a high level of sophistication. 'This life of Lucknow was sweet and gracious' wrote one historian, 'free from worldly cares and anxieties.' It flourished through the 19th and at least part of the 20th century and crumbled with the blows of history: among them, the Partition of India, which caused many to emigrate to Pakistan and the abolition of the Zamindari system. When Urdu was replaced by Hindi, as practical and needed as that move may have been, it wiped out an entire vocabulary of life.

For Nina, the very atmosphere in the Lucknow of the 1930s and 40s, the grace of its etiquette and courteous manner of speech, the experience of life lived once again amidst music, was almost intoxicating, the slaking of her thirst. She enjoyed their visits to the city; there was an air of *nazakat*, delicacy, to everything, not forgetting food. Awadh, after all, was where poultry used to be fed on jasmine and pomegranate to flavour the meat, where in the past, skilled chefs would compete with each other to pull off the most amazing *trompe l'oeils* by making a meat curry look like a light *murabba* or conserve. And what appeared to be a khichri of rice and lentil would actually be an appetizing savoury made with almonds cut to look like grains of rice and pistachios like lentils. The fancifully named '*labh-e-mashooqa*', or lips of the beloved, was an exotic confection of cream, honey, spices and almonds with betel nut to add the red colour; for the Nawab, however, the red came from the powdered rubies that were mixed in especially for him. The spiced biryani of Delhi gave way here to the more subtle pulao of which there were seven major variations with enticing names like *gulzar*, the garden, or *noor*, the light. A speciality was a dish called *mutanjan*, made of meat and rice with sugar and spices. The houses of the aristocracy and the *taluqdars* were renowned for serving the finest of foods and Pamela's home, Prasada Bhawan in Shahjahanpur, was famous through the region for its superb cuisine.

Nina's heart, so conditioned by the influence of her grandfather Keshub Chandra Sen, responded to the syncretic nature of the legacy of the Nawabs, who understood that Muslim practices and Hindu practices could be harmonized. Asaf-ud-Daula (who reigned from 1775–1797) gave a large grant for the building of a Hanuman temple; he joined in the festivals of Holi and Diwali to play with colours and lights. It was an attitude that did not make Hindus and Muslims conflicting binaries, but two distinct forms of expression of certain truths which had many things in common and many things not in common. Much later, Nawab Wajid Ali Shah followed this tradition of tolerance and said, 'All ills come from ignorance, it is through knowledge of one another's culture that communities learn to respect each other.' And he followed his own saying: when he was young, he staged a play in 1843 that he himself had directed about Radha and Krishna. This was a moment to be marked, for it was the first time that a Muslim king had staged a play about a Hindu god. A few years later, in the palace of Kaisarbagh, he would stage rahas, or dramatic musical productions mostly about Radha, Krishna and the *gopis*, and appear himself in front of an admiring public in the role of Krishna, his body coloured blue with a powder of finely ground turquoise and pearls.

Richly caparisoned elephant with Prasada Bhawan in the background

Nina revelled in this city, the 'bride of India', which seemed to be an echo of her own being, with its spiritual wealth of temples, mosques, and its imambaras raised by Shia rulers. She found herself increasingly attracted to its Islamic traditions, the mystic faith of the Sufis with its message of '*Sulh-e-Kul*', peace to all, its inclusivity and the devotional music of the ecstatic qawwali heard in the dargahs. Yet here also was the music of *shringar*: the worldly romance of the *thumri*, the *dadra*, the ghazal, with their haunting cries of love and yearning; expressed also in the poetry and dance that were part of the life of Lucknow.

In the house in Lucknow she sought to revive an old tradition of music; this, after all, was where Bade Sarkar used to have *mujras*, the private concerts where the famous *baijis* of Lucknow would entertain a male audience with their singing and dancing. These concerts were usually held to mark occasions such as weddings or the birth of a child, also festivals like Holi and

Dussehra. Women could not publicly attend, so they watched and listened from the women's quarters or from behind screens, the *chilmans* that hid their presence. Now she insisted that Rip revive this tradition by holding *mujras* in their home; certainly this must have shocked people (as she once confessed in an interview) but she insisted nevertheless. Rip must have responded positively to such requests; he himself loved listening to good singers and was only too aware of his wife's hunger for music.

During each performance, Nina would listen intently from behind the *chilman*, soaking in every nuance of the rendition of songs, the gestures and expressions. And after the performance, she would send for the *baiji* and speak to her, noting down the essential details of all the songs: the words, the ragas, specific textures and colours that determined when and how they would be sung, the names of the poets. Her alert ears were quick to pick up and replicate the subtleties of Urdu diction, the degree of weight or lightness of syllable and vowel from which meaning was drawn. And the sweetness of Purabi, language of the heartland, for a variety of seasonal songs, the amorous languor of *chaiti* of the early summer and the sorrowful separation of *kajri* when heavy rains kept lovers apart. A large part of the repertoire that she carefully built up over the years and used for her own performances, and then later taught her students, was sourced from these occasions.

Such performances probably sparked off what was to be her life-long interest in the figure of the the *tawaif*, the *baiji*, the courtesan. We could certainly question why she, a lady from a privileged background, would concern herself so deeply with women completely outside her social ambit. But she herself gives a passionate explanation in a paper that she wrote:

> ...Thumri is more suited to the female voice, perhaps this is the reason why this form of music was practised by courtesans, Tawaifs and Baijis from Banaras, Lucknow and Gaya. It enabled them to musically emote the overwhelming injustice of their third class status as artistes and human beings, and also act as spokeswomen for their more economically privileged sisters imprisoned in the zenana, whose menfolk come to the kothas for an evening of diversion and entertainment.

This paper, entitled 'Women in Traditional Media', was written in 1991 for a national consultation in Bangalore whose overarching theme was 'Empowering Women through Media'. We can see that just over half a century separates the experience of actually listening to the *tawaifs* from behind the *chilman* and then speaking about them to a packed hall in South India. Her language is strong, with key words like 'injustice' and 'imprisoned'; they sound as if they have been wrenched from some deeply-felt interior space. It is the collective memory of her own music and its denial, of all the women who faced such heavy odds in the practice of their art.

By the time this address was given, the archetypal *tawaif* had all but disappeared from the music scene, and the riches of that repertoire now belonged to accomplished professional concert singers who, in a later and kinder age, were permitted to sing in public without stigma and with dignity. But to better understand the prevailing social environment and her individual response to it, that paper is reproduced at the end of this book. And it is a fact that her strongly-voiced feeling of injustice persisted, and many years later inspired her friend and fellow music connoisseur, Pran Neville, to write the book *Nautch Girls of India* which describes the state of the women who were condemned by society.

The *tawaifs* and *baijis* whose music Nina heard in Lucknow were even then, in the first half of the 20th century, part of a brave but fading tradition. That tradition had reached its zenith with the nawabs of Lucknow and more specifically Wajid Ali Shah. '…the courtesans were an influential female elite…' writes one historian of that time, and none more so than those of Awadh. The best of them were sought after and admired, adept in music and dance, could recite poetry, and had the gifts of both coquetry and articulation to carry on a sparkling conversation in the *mehfil* or gathering. They were free to enter into relationships as they chose from amongst the circles of wealthy men who surrounded them. They used good will—and money—for the advancement of their friends to high places and thus cemented their own place in the spheres of influence; and '…it was said that until a person had associations with courtesans he was not a polished man.' Young male offspring of the aristocracy were often sent to them to acquire the skills of social etiquette and the discernment to appreciate the best of literature and poetry. They were the keepers of the polite, refined culture of Awadh.

Some of the women were wealthy enough to be tax payers and property owners in their own right; and they could also be very powerful women, like Wajid Ali Shah's wife, Begum Hazrat Mahal who played an important role in the Great Uprising of 1857 and placed her son, Birjis Qadr, temporarily on the throne.

Rani Nina—a formal portrait

Alas, it was that very same Uprising that brought them down. After the siege of their Residency in Lucknow and the subsequent retaking of the city, the British were in a savage and vindictive frame of mind. They thought—and perhaps not without reason—that the *kothas* of the *tawaifs* had played some part in the rebellion, that at the very least these houses were meeting places for conspiracies to be worked out with the help of the *tawaifs*, whose connections with the feudal landlords were only too well-known. A lot of their properties were seized, and they were branded as common prostitutes. In the aftermath of the Great Uprising, and as the courtesans tried to resume their heritage and pick up the pieces, many of the certainties they took for granted were splintered: the court was gone, many of their patrons were gone, the entire social scene that had made them relevant was vanishing. A new wave of moral reformists dubbed them as sinful symbols of decadence.

Yet they managed to survive. In the late 19th century the new art of photography captured their bejewelled images for posterity, sitting pensively in large chairs or fetchingly arranged against bolsters, some with elaborate paan boxes and hookahs by their side. And in the early 20th century they were the first musicians to be recorded for the gramophone. This not only kept their art alive but also took it to larger and wider audiences.

The move to get new 'listening ears' for other genres of music also got an impetus from the august figure of Vishnu Narayan Bhatkhande. Apart from being a prolific writer on music and the author of an exhaustive classification system of ragas, he was the tireless organizer of musical conferences in various cities which presented great performers to the general public. In 1926 he established the Marris College of Music in Lucknow—named after the then Governor Sir William Marris—which was later renamed the Bhatkhande Music Institute and still later upgraded to a Deemed University. Lucknow was now becoming a centre of music once again, and the power and sheer reach of radio were added with the opening of the All India Radio station in 1938. It was here at the radio station that Nina caught up with her old friend and fellow music student, her guru-bhai Sunil Bose, now a senior member of its staff.

Pandit Vishnu Narayan Bhatkande

What a happy encounter that must have been! For as long as Nina and Rip continued their winter visits to Lucknow, they kept in touch with Sunil Bose, often going to his house for small impromptu concerts, where they would sing the familiar *thumris* that had been taught by Girija Babu and laugh as they remembered the old days of carefree joy. Surely Rip must have seen how Nina blossomed in this atmosphere, how these informal exchanges of music satisfied a kind of hunger within her that nothing else could. And surely that is precisely why he encouraged her to record music with the Columbia Record Company, which she did, cutting her first record with two *dadras*. It is inconceivable that she recorded under the name of Rani Nina Ripjit Singh; it also seems impossible that her father-in-law had any knowledge of this and it is almost certain that she used the name by which the world would later know her—Naina Devi.

Changing Lives

Around her the world had changed and continued to change at an accelerating pace. A World War had taken place, and the invincibility of an Imperial power had been challenged and found wanting. The Raj was palpably nearing its end, and Simla and its character had altered.

In 1943 Lord Linlithgow, a man described by Pandit Nehru as '...solid as a rock with almost a rock's lack of awareness...' was succeeded as Viceroy by Lord Wavell. The latter had earlier been Commander-in-Chief in India and was quite aware of the political situation in India and the many pitfalls it presented. The move towards self-governance was entering a decisive phase; but it was deadlocked and a new set of discussions had to be held on its modalities. Whatever was worked out had to be acceptable to both the Congress and the Muslim League, and that was Wavell's most important

task. Finally in 1945 the Simla Conference was convened between the Viceroy and the most important political leaders of India to present and discuss the Wavell Plan. In brief, it proposed the formation of an interim government before taking up the work of framing the Constitution; this government was to be a balanced proportionate representation of the main communities, including the Muslims and 'Caste Hindus' (this term being greatly resented by Mahatma Gandhi). And there would be a new Executive Council in which all members except the Viceroy and the Commander-in-Chief would be Indians. This Executive Council was also temporary, until such time as a new Constitution could be agreed upon and put into force. All portfolios except Defence would be held by Indian members.

Wavell might have thought that he was presenting a fair proposal, but from the outset the effort was thwarted by the unhappy dynamics between groups and factions: Hindus and Muslims, Congress and Muslim League: and a general atmosphere of suspicion and distrust. The idea of a separate state for Muslims was already swirling around. In Allahabad, addressing a session of the All India Muslim League in 1930, Allama Iqbal (the poet who wrote '*Sare Jahan Se Accha*') had already said, 'I therefore demand the formation of a consolidated Muslim State in the best interests of India and Islam...' The talks broke down on the issue of the selection of Muslim representatives, and who would do it—the Muslim League, which projected itself as the sole voice of Indian Muslims, or the Congress which claimed the position as the larger and pan-Indian party with many Muslim members, and finally no agreement could be reached.

But now the situation in Britain had changed; an election had swept the Labour party into power in 1945 and they wished to transfer power to Indians as fast as possible; devastated by a long-drawn-out war, they could no longer maintain their empire. A Cabinet Mission of three senior ministers was dispatched to India, and once again Simla was the hub for the meetings between the ministers and all the important political leaders. The Mission's Plan envisaged, among other things, that there would be a united dominion of India based on a confederation of provinces, and these provinces would be clustered by religion, those of the North West, Assam and parts of Bengal being Muslim majority and those of central and southern India being Hindu majority. A central government in Delhi would handle overarching national matters such as defence and foreign affairs. Again, there was dissent and disagreement between the two main players; the sequence of events that followed included acute political antagonism, communal violence and killings, and in early 1947 the British Government decided to wash their hands of the matter by fixing June 1948 as the final date for the transfer of power to one—or more than one if no solution to the impasse could be found—government.

Wavell was now replaced as Viceroy by Lord Louis Mountbatten, after which events proceeded so fast that they seem like a speeded-up film. Within months of his arrival in spring 1947, Mountbatten had ruthlessly cut the Gordian knot and proposed the Partition of India into two independent dominions, following which the British Parliament passed the Indian Independence Act 1947 that received Royal Assent in July 1947. The date of June 1948 was summarily advanced to August 1947, and the borders of the new countries were hastily pencilled in by a man named Cyril Radcliffe who did not know very much about India and worked with out-of-date maps and materials. The immense tragedy of Partition with its huge cost in human terms is too well known to need recounting, but it still raises some questions, among them, had Mountbatten not been in such a hurry, would the outcomes have been different?

These were times of incredible upheavals on the national scale and some of that action had played out in the town of Simla. What the response was from Raja Charanjit Singh, we do not know, nor whether he was involved in any way as a Member of the Council of State but surely he, Rip and Nina were all conscious that their world was turning in a different direction.

But the biggest upheaval for them was about to come two years after Independence, and its effect would be violent and very personal for each one of them: it would disrupt all their lives forever. For some time, Rip's

health had been causing concern. The best medical advice was sought and an opinion expressed that living at an altitude was unsuitable for him, and that it would be better if his summers were no longer spent in Simla. Perhaps that annual cycle of going up and down from and to the plains had upset his blood pressure. Dr Heilig, a noted cardiologist consulted in Jaipur, referred him to Dr B.C. Roy, one of the best known physicians in Calcutta, a city where he would also be under the loving care of Nina's family. Rip and Nina left for Calcutta in August and while he was undergoing treatment they had a quiet celebration for their wedding anniversary. Fourteen years! How the time had flown! It had been a time of happiness, protected by the love and warmth of an indulgent husband.

The very next day a message came from Rip's father saying that he wanted them to return immediately to Simla. It was decided that Nina would leave but Rip would stay on for a few more days. Back in Simla, Nina received a telegram saying that Rip had taken ill and that she should come to Calcutta. Alarmed, she left for Delhi from where she flew to Calcutta. But it was too late. Rip was already dead of a cerebral haemorrhage caused by a massive and sudden rise in his blood pressure.

Nina's world turned upside down. After the shock and pain, her first thought was for her children, her daughters Nilika and Rena who were in school in Lucknow, her older son Ratanjit (Reggie) at the Welham Preparatory School in Dehradun and her youngest, Karanjit (Kenny), who was only three years old. And for Raja Charanjit Singh, it was a terrible loss that he could not speak about. His youngest son and the only one to stay by his side was gone. But there was no exhibition of grief, no crying, it was a loss that became a deep internal wound.

Wounded people are vulnerable people, easily influenced, and he was no different. It was not long before whispers, insinuations and intrigue floated about like malignant clouds, and they all centred around Nina. Nina was young, she was beautiful, her whole life was still ahead of her. What might she do next? What if...what if...she remarried? What would become of the children? What if she took them away? And what about the properties? Once again, it was Charanjit Singh's brother-in-law who filled his head with sinister scenarios and his ears with poison. Perhaps he himself was being cleverly manipulated.

Nina, already broken by grief, found it difficult to understand the growing hostility at Chapslee, the undercurrents that seemed to swirl around. It was a situation that was becoming more and more difficult to deal with; her period of mourning was not allowed to be one of sorrowful meditation and a quiet coming to terms with the reality of loss. Instead it was a turmoil, a maelstrom of antagonism and she felt an incomprehensible malevolence in the air. This was not the safe, secure Chapslee she had known for over a decade.

Then another blow was dealt. Her father-in-law now wanted custody of the children, something that was completely, totally, out of the question. She was adamant in her refusal, she would never sign her children away. She moved to Rajanagar for the winter where she found that a second kitchen was being built. The new kitchen was going to be hers, and the food that would be made for her would be different to the food being cooked for Raja sahib. It was puzzling, but then she found out that the Raja sahib had been told that Nina had bribed the cook to poison him.

She could not believe this at first, believe that anyone could even say or think this, or that her father-in-law would give this accusation more than the merest moment of his attention before dismissing it. It was beyond credibility, and the hurt was a deep blow. It was as if the last fourteen years of belonging, of loyalty, of loving, of service, had been wiped away and as if she remained an outsider of dubious intent. Now she heard that he had been told, and believed, that in some way she was exploiting him. Each new accusation was like an assault, and hurt her deeply. She could not understand why this was happening.

But all these were matters that she kept to herself. They could not be discussed with anyone else, not with her own family (who in any case

were already occupied dealing with the problem of Sadhona); nor with friends who, however close they were, remained outsiders to the family. It would be a betrayal of sorts if she spoke about such private family matters with anyone.

At what point does a spirit finally break before it can be healed again? These were very dark days for Nina, so dark that she descended into a deep depression. Life did not seem worth living, death would be a merciful escape. Her health began to deteriorate and finally she had to be rushed to hospital where an empathetic Civil Surgeon took her under his care. He spoke reassuringly to her: 'Nina, you will be alright, don't worry about your children, don't worry about anything, we are all here…' and slowly her equilibrium was restored.

This was a situation where suspicion and intrigue had wrecked relationships to the point where they could no longer be sustained. There was too much hostility, even with Pamela whom she had loved so dearly and that hurt her very much. A separation seemed to be in the best interests of all, for which practical arrangements had to be made. It was agreed that Nina would retain custody of the children, and that their vacations (all of them being in boarding school) would be spent half with their grandfather and half with their mother. And Nina was made to sign a statement that declared that she had received her legally entitled share of everything in her lifetime and that nothing more was due to her.

It is interesting that many years later Charanjit Singh told his grandson Kenny (Karanjit) that he did that to protect all of them. He always thought that Nina would marry again and he wanted to make sure that nobody could take away the rights of his grandchildren. But at that time it was decided that Nina would stay in Rajanagar. For the moment, the assets and the staff were divided between her and her father-in-law: tractors, cars, farm equipment, managers and munshis, drivers and workers and there was a clear split of the proceeds, the agricultural produce. It was a temporary measure, because he moved to Bareilly shortly after that and then pursued his own life, occasionally returning to Rajanagar for visits but never to stay for long.

Nina continued to live in Rajanagar. But the truth was she had no money. And Rajanagar, which had been her happy rural idyll with Rip, was a stand-alone estate, no place for a woman on her own. There was no electricity, nor a neighbour in sight, and safety was an issue. True, Pamela was not far away but now things were different between them. She began to realize that her life was all in her own hands, it was she and she alone who had to chart her future and that of her children, and it could not be here in Rajanagar. Finally she went to Delhi to meet her old friend, Sharda, who, in a golden age long ago, had welcomed her as a bride when she arrived at Simla Railway Station and who was now Sharda Rao. It so happened that her husband, C.B. Rao, was the Director General of All India Radio, and a connoisseur of music. Both husband and wife had heard Nina sing at the very rare private and impromptu *mehfils* held for a limited inner social circle, and both had appreciated the quality of her voice, its sweetness and clarity. Their advice was robustly given: 'You have a wonderful talent, Nina, such a beautiful voice. That talent can rebuild your life and if you do not use it, you will lose your sanity. You must sing.'

Such strong positive words. They were a healing balm for the damage caused by cruelty; they restored her battered confidence and strengthened her will to pick up the pieces and put herself together again. She auditioned successfully for All India Radio and travelled from Rajanagar to Delhi for recordings.

Call it destiny, good luck, or what you will, it seemed as if the Raos had re-entered her life as guardian angels to guide her on an onward course. C.B. Rao was a senior officer of the ICS. He was not only a bureaucrat, but a Hindi poet; and the Rao home was like a salon where renowned poets of the day, such as Harivansh Rai Bachchan, Maithili Sharan Gupt, Sumitra Nandan Pant and Ramdhari Singh 'Dinkar', all met for sparkling exchanges of word play and recitations of their latest work. It was C.B. Rao who re-christened All India Radio as Akashvani, a term at once imaginative and appropriate. This love for Hindi poetry might well have stemmed from his upbringing in Allahabad as the son of Sir C.Y. Chintamani, who was for

a long time the Editor of *The Leader*, the premier newspaper of the city started by Madan Mohan Malviya.

Sharda Rao had studied Hindi at Indraprastha College in Delhi and was married immediately after that. But when the family came back to Delhi in the early 1950s, she too wished to take up a job and joined the Government in the Ministry of Education's Hindi Division and later, the Ministry of Scientific Research and Cultural Affairs. Amongst the portfolios entrusted to her as Joint Education Advisor were the newly created institutions of culture: the Sangeet Natak Akademi, the Sahitya Akademi and the Lalit

Mrs Sharda Rao; her friendship and advice helped Naina Devi at a critical time

Kala Akademi. Her role was that of an administrative and supervisory head, and the experience gave her deep insights into the cultural world.

Both were of immense help to Nina as it was becoming increasingly clear that her future lay in Delhi, but before she could make this definitive move, she had to take care of a number of things. A priority was the wedding of her older daughter, Nilika, which took place in Chapslee in 1953. Nina had a constant problem of money looming over her head, but she managed to take care of matters somehow. Once her youngest, Kenny, went to boarding school, she dealt with Rajanagar by giving away some 300 acres of land to Vinoba Bhave's Bhoodan movement.

On one visit to Delhi, Sharda Rao had introduced her to a friend, Mrs Sumitra Charat Ram, who was about to set up a cultural institute in the capital and looking for a Director to manage it. It was a perfect fit for Nina and now at last it was time for her to move out and move on.

NAINA DEVI

DELHI: 1953–1993

Naina Devi

Why did she adopt the name of Naina Devi? The story of how and why she chose this name has been told many times; she herself recounted it in some of her writings and interviews. But it bears repetition, not only as a re-defining of her essential and individual identity but also as a poignant reminder of how she turned to this name for anonymity in her time of need. One of her interviewers gave this interpretation, '...a brief memory from the past flared up in her. The memory of an old woman in the first wash of light over the oldest city in the universe... and a plaintive *thumri* that flowed with the great river, taking her from one truth to a greater truth.'

This observation is as acute as it is poetically expressed. From the deepest recesses of her memory came the haunting images and sounds of her childhood when her mother used to take her to Benaras (now Varanasi) to visit her grandmother who lived there. Early in the morning her grandmother used to go to the Ahilyabai Ghat to bathe in the Ganga, accompanied by little Nilina; and while she bathed, the child sat on the steps of the ghat gazing up at the alcove where a beggar woman lived. She was fascinated by that old woman; by her shorn hair, which brought into focus her large and expressive eyes; by her white sari, which marked her out as one who had renounced all and given up the world. Most of all, she was fascinated by the song she used to sing to the river,

'Hey Govind, hey Gopal, suniye Prabhu mori
Hey Govind rakho sharan ab to jeevan hare.'

It was a plaintive cry from the heart. 'Help me, my Lord, give me your protection for I have lost the will to live.' Who was this woman so sang

Naina Devi photographed at the peak of her activities with Raag Rang

so beautifully, with such devastating truth in her voice? Later, she found out that the beggar woman was once a well-known *tawaif* of Benaras who had chosen to turn her back on her material existence to seek her salvation through renunciation. 'This left an indelible impact on my mind,' she wrote. 'I could not sing under my own name because I did not want to offend my family members; so I sang incognito under the pseudonym Naina Devi ...I decided to take the name...after her beautiful sad eyes.'

Sad and beautiful the context might have been, but in the following four decades Naina Devi achieved the rare heights which belong to only those people who find at last what they have sought for so long. Perhaps the greater truth she realized was that to gain something you have to lose something, that when she took on the mantle of Naina Devi, the lady known as Rani Nina Ripjit Singh would recede into the background. That persona would be gently peeled away in the same way that she had shed herself of so many of her belongings and given away her expensive clothes and beautiful jewellery. We could surmise that this was not an issue for her, because the events of the past months had shown in a very stark manner how much could vanish in the blink of an eye, how foundations could be removed from under you and the only foundation worth having was the one you built for yourself with your own passion and your own work.

The Bharatiya Kala Kendra

The situation she was about to enter in New Delhi had enjoyed a fortunate confluence of elements: the post-Independence cultural revival, the visionaries who were in the right place at the right time to sustain its future, and the moments of history that shaped a new national capital into a cultural capital. Through the good offices of Sharda Rao, she had met Mrs Sumitra Charat Ram, the wife of well-known industrialist Charat Ram, who, along

with her collaborator Nirmala Joshi, was about to regenerate an artistic atmosphere in the city. Already in the years before Independence the connoisseur and arts activist Nirmala Joshi had established the Delhi School for Hindustani Music and Dance—which later became the Sangeet Bharati—bringing several renowned artistes to the city as teachers for its students. The Kathak maestro Acchan Maharaj (father of Birju Maharaj) was among them and his list of pupils included Sitara Devi and Damayanti Joshi.

Mrs Sumitra Charat Ram of the Bharatiya Kala Kendra

Mrs Charat Ram herself had grown up in a family environment that encouraged education for girls and artistic pursuits. Before she was married, she had visited the Uday Shankar School in Almora and observed closely its methods and techniques and how an art was transmitted from teacher to pupil. For her, it was an experience that left a lasting impression; apart from meeting legendary artistes at close quarters, it gave her insights about how such an activity could proceed in an organized manner.

But it was a single event which precipitated the long association between the two women. On Independence Day in 1947, Sumitra Charat Ram decided to celebrate the occasion with a concert which was held in the family home on Curzon Road. No invitations were issued, but somehow through word of mouth a sizable number of people turned up. They were treated to a whole night of unforgettable music by the most eminent musicians of the day: Pandit Ravi Shankar (in fact, it was he who had suggested the event), Ustad Allauddin Khan, Ustad Hafiz Ali Khan, Ustad Vilayat Khan, Ustad Faiyaz Khan and Pandit Pannalal Ghosh, among others. It was a uniquely Indian concert held in a very anglicized city during the dying throes of the Imperial Raj; a city where, perhaps, people had forgotten their own roots. The response to the concert, however, showed that there were many music lovers in Delhi, and so the Jhankar Music Circle was formed, whose members included both Sumitra Charat Ram and Nirmala Joshi as well as Pandit Ravi Shankar, the Nawab of Pataudi and Pandit Haksar. A number of rare musical events—such as a presentation which brought together in stunning simultaneous performance the sitars of Pandit Ravi Shankar and Ustad Vilayat Khan, and the sarod of Ustad Ali Akbar Khan—were staged with great success, for audiences whose interest was revived by this informal yet intense communication between them and the musicians. The two ladies worked together for the organization and presentation of these events, and their bonds of trust and friendship grew.

Nirmala Joshi's energy and enthusiasm were boundless, and she went on to create the Bharatiya Kala Kendra in in 1952. Here again, music and dance were to be taught, and the Government supported its efforts with a modest grant of Rs 20,000. Before long, however, an Act of Parliament instituted the Sangeet Natak Akademi, which was to be the National Academy for Dance and Music, and Nirmala Joshi was appointed as its first Secretary. She realized immediately that this huge task was going to absorb all the time and energy she had, so she suggested to Sumitra Charat Ram that she take over the Kendra and its day-to-day running. Perhaps Mrs Charat Ram viewed the prospect with trepidation; perhaps also she saw in it not only the challenges she would have to face, but more importantly, the great contribution she could make on a national basis. The list of an early Governing Council includes many distinguished names, such as Mrs Indira Gandhi as Chairman of the Executive Committee with Mrs Charat Ram as Secretary and Mrs Rukmini Devi Arundale, Mrs Sharda Rao and Begum Qudsia Zaidi, amongst others, as Members. As it happened, during the next decades the Kendra grew under her guidance, not just as a school for training in the performing arts but also a fertile ground for creativity in a number of allied disciplines like choreography, especially in Kathak.

The growth of the Bharatiya Kala Kendra (later renamed the Shriram Bharatiya Kala Kendra) was made possible by the weight of the sheer talent that gathered there, both those who taught and those who learnt. The

dancer Maya Rao was selected to come to Delhi on a scholarship after her audition in the Marris College of Music in Lucknow (now the Bhatkhande University) where one of the examiners was Nirmala Joshi. She was going to be the first pupil of the Kathak legend, Shambhu Maharaj, a charismatic dancer who had also learnt the art of *thumri* singing from Ustad Rahimuddin. Audiences were held spellbound when he sat on the stage to sing in his mellow voice and act out the words from his seemingly inexhaustible vocabulary of abhinaya or bhava. He was brought from Lucknow to teach at the Kendra.

Simply to accommodate the artistes and their classrooms posed problems in the early days, but the situation was taken care of with some improvisation and a 'can-do' attitude. However, sometimes this did not work and some cajoling was needed. In her autobiography, *Maya Rao: A Lifetime in Choreography*, the dancer recalled:

> For the first ten months, the Bharatiya Kala Kendra did not possess their private space. In the interim, my classes were sometimes at Nirmalaji's office in the Akademi or at Sumitraji's house on Curzon Road and this continued till the Institute rented a space on Pusa Road. The Shriram Mansion was huge with over thirty rooms. Nirmalaji appointed Govind Vidhyarthiji to oversee our classes. Since it was Sumitraji's home, we had to move our classes from one room to another each day, depending on the family's whims. This would provoke a moody Shambhu Maharaji, who would suddenly throw a tantrum saying he did not want to teach in a dark room or move to the verandah of the house. Govindji with his calm demeanour would always be around to pacify him. For this reason, Govindji was labelled as a shock absorber.

The House on Pusa Road

It was to 5 B Pusa Road, a house hired for the activities of the Bharatiya Kala Kendra, where Naina Devi came when she was appointed as its Resident Director. She stayed in one part of the building, where she was allotted two rooms, a space that had to include her children when they came from their schools. It was certainly not Chapslee, but it was a home of her very own and it was endless music. Fitting in was a bit of a squeeze; one of the two

Old friends: (L to R) Naina Devi, Pandit Mallikarjun Mansur, Ustad Amjad Ali Khan, Mrs Sumitra Charat Ram, Mrs Shobha Deepak Singh

rooms was used as a sitting room and office and the other as a bedroom and dining area where every inch of space, including storage space, was used to the best effect. The annexe was where the sarod maestro, Ustad Hafiz Ali Khan, stayed with his sons, Rahmat Ali Khan and Amjad Ali Khan—later to become a brilliant musician and eminent sarod player in his own right. The rest of the house, including the covered terrace and the courtyard at the back, hummed with music and dance and the artistic soirees that were the activities of the Kendra.

An informal *mehfil* at home. The galaxy of musicians includes tabla maestro Samta Prasad (foreground) surrounded by Ustad Vilayat Khan, a young Shujaat Khan, Ustad Fahimuddin Dagar, Ustad Asad Ali Khan, Ustad Yunus Hussain Khan and Ustad Ghulam Sadiq Khan, amongst others

It was a dazzling array of teachers who gathered there: the senior Dagar brothers, Ustad Nasir Moinuddin and Nasir Aminuddin Khan sahibs, Ustad Mushtaq Hussain Khan, Ustad Vilayat Husain Khan, Vidushi Siddheshwari Devi, Ustad Ishtiaq Hussain Khan, Ustad Hafiz Ali Khan of course, and the Kathak masters, Guru Shambhu Maharaj and Guru Sundar Prasad. For generations the great artistes of northern India had been sustained by the patronage of royal courts and affluent zamindars; it was here that their art had been nurtured, as patrons took care of their livelihoods and their families and encouraged them to transmit their skills to their own children. By the mid-20th century the system had been collapsing for many decades and was on the verge of extinction. It was the cultural institutions of the post-Independence era that now took on the role of enabling performers to teach their art to a young generation, one that was not necessarily from their own families.

The great teachers attracted highly talented pupils: in Kathak, for example, it was dancers like Maya Rao, Kumudini Lakhia, Uma Sharma, Rani Karna and Shovana Narayan who went on to be acclaimed across the country for both their dancing as well as their progressive choreography.

Apart from teachers and their pupils, the Kendra, like all institutions, needed constant support and supervision from the committed visionaries who helped to guide it into the future. In this Naina Devi's role has always been acknowledged. She was an essential part of a threesome that worked closely together. Nirmala Joshi would develop or create a concept, which would then be taken further and implemented by Naina Devi and then, as Sumitra Charat Ram modestly said, 'I helped financially'. Nainaji would often call to suggest that the Kendra host an artiste passing through Delhi, and in this manner it became a centre where musicians and dancers could meet informally and share their experiences.

One of her most important contributions was her empathetic dealings with the artistes; creative talents of that calibre are very sensitive and need a special understanding. It helped that she herself was a singer; she had experienced the stresses of continuous practice and the tensions and apprehensions that any artiste has before a performance. Her instinct as a musician guided her to discern what a particular person needed or wanted and in that sense she was the bridge between Sumitra Charat Ram as the patron and the growing number of artistes who were drawn to the Kendra. This was an important contribution, and it often went further when she drew from her own training and repertoire to suggest gently to a musician what he or she might sing, a particular raga, or a seasonal song. Such were the areas where she could communicate with artistes on familiar ground, common to both, which built up a special rapport. It was the basis for mutual trust and confidence, a critical need for any institute when it begins and starts to grow.

Overall there was a strong sense of friendship and of a family working together. The three women would sit together and sip cold coffee as they

discussed plans for the future or specifics of the execution of some imminent programme. That one of them was being paid a salary by the other did not upset the status quo of friendship nor impose a set of hierarchies.

But despite the exhilaration of the present and the joy of being in an environment of such creativity, of course there were reminders of the past, how could there not be, and one was the sheer physicality of her situation, the two rooms, the constricted space. There was the memory of Chapslee, all those rooms, those chandeliers, the tapestries, the gardens. Closer by, the memory of Akbar Road and the splendid bungalow in the heart of the new city. Then the reality of that cramped area. She put a brave face on it; her children were still young; they had already seen her journey through despair, and for their sake she must make light of any difficulties they faced individually or as a family. She could give them little by way of material comforts, but she could give them the gifts of joy and laughter and togetherness.

For the children it juxtaposed two sharply opposing ends of a spectrum. The one half of the holidays they spent with their grandfather was like the old familiar Chapslee in some ways: the regulated life, the spacious comfort, staff to look after their every need. And yet over it hung a cloud of sadness and grief: the loss of their father and now the absence of their mother. In Delhi when they were with their mother, they were all crammed into that small space, there was no transport, and they all learnt to travel in autos and pay the fare of four annas to Connaught Place. There was a tremendous disparity to cope with, and a great many new things to learn.

And yet.

First of all, they were happy to be with their mother. Their home was wherever she was and they could see that she was happy in this new atmosphere. There was much laughter as they slipped into a completely different environment, one where the surroundings were filled with musicians and dancers, who wandered in and out of their rooms or who were met in other rooms of the house, artistes like Ustad Hafiz Ali Khan sahib and Shambhu

With Octavio Paz, poet and Nobel Laureate, the Mexican Ambassador to India in the 1960s (centre). They are flanked by Ustad Vilayat Khan (left) and Rena Ripjit Singh (right)

Maharaj. Maybe they were too young, too untutored, to realize then the exceptional calibre of their new neighbours, or the great esteem in which they were held. But they did learn a social truth from their mother: how to perceive people not through the prism of pedigree or status but as humans and valuable in their own right, especially if they had a talent which they gifted to society. It was a period of adjustments, some fast, some slow, some previously unthinkable: but they all managed to pull through.

The adjustment, however, did not include social adjustments. Changing her life and her home did not mean losing her friends. All the friends and contacts that she had made, whether in Chapslee or in Akbar Road, continued to keep in touch. Sometimes there would be discreet little parties where, after hours and when there was no soiree on the premises, the work table would be re-set and seating arranged somehow to entertain the her old contacts—Princess Sita of Kapurthala, Rani sahib Faridkot amongst others—and they came to meet her. It was a part of her life which was somewhat different from

At a party, Princess Sita of Kapurthala (left of Naina Devi), General Mishri Chand (on sofa arm) and other old friends

At a social evening with General Thimayya, then Chief of the Army Staff

the one that she shared with the musicians, yet she wove it in seamlessly; it is to the credit of both sides that neither seemed to care for the trappings of formality but only for a warm social presence; and these connections lasted through her life, no matter where she stayed.

Pusa Road was the first and smallest of Naina Devi's homes in Delhi. The next home was the site of the Ferozeshah Road hutments, and it was a larger space. She would go through many more homes in the city, in Jangpura, in Birbal Road, in Vinay Marg, before coming at last to her final home in Kaka Nagar. Each of her homes was an open house for her friends, especially musicians and more especially those who needed shelter and caring through periods of ill-health. Ustad Bade Ghulam Ali Khan and Ustad Vilayat Khan were amongst the many who stayed with her as they recuperated from ailments; often the invalids were accompanied by spouses and other family members during the process to recovery. Sometimes they stayed for weeks or months. It did not seem to matter to Naina Devi; her space was an

elastic one which swelled magically with need. Her primary concern was the wellbeing of the artiste. When the children were with her, they sometimes had to vacate their rooms to accommodate the others and sometimes they had to share. Kenny once woke up to find himself looking at the face of a total stranger in the next bed. 'I nearly had a heart attack!' he said. But then, he knew his mother well, and so went right back to sleep.

Ustad Mushtaq Hussain Khan and the Bareilly Sharif

In the second half of the 1950s, the teaching staff of the Bharatiya Kala Kendra was joined by the great singer, Ustad Mushtaq Hussain Khan of the Rampur-Sahaswan gharana, and Naina Devi used this opportunity to become a student again. She learnt (or re-learnt) the form of khayal, and surely it must have evoked memories of her youthful days in Calcutta and those hours spent perfecting musical phrases under the guidance of Girija Babu. She knew then that she was past the age and stage of learning where she could do any justice to the performance of khayal, but she saw this process as a means of adding a vocal training and musical discipline to her *thumri* singing that would strengthen its foundation and enhance its richness.

It is tempting to speculate what her Ustad, Mushtaq Hussain Khan, made of her desire to learn from him. It had its ironic aspect because he himself steadfastly refused to sing *thumri* publicly though he taught it to his students; and the very idea that *thumri* was a beautiful and ornamental counterpoint to the austerity of khayal gayaki would have been rejected by him with some ferocity. In this he was not alone. Other maestros like Amir Khan did not sing the form in public, whereas some, like Ustad Faiyaz Khan and Bade Ghulam Ali Khan, did, and were heavily criticized for it. Mushtaq Hussain Khan, in common with many other male musicians of that era, regarded *thumri* as music fit only for *tawaifs*; once, in Aligarh University at the end of his recital he was besieged by requests for *thumri*, to which his stern reply was, '*Main koi rundee nahin hoon*' (I am not a prostitute). Surely he must have been quite aware of Naina Devi's love of *thumri* and her expansive repertoire in the genre. Yet between them there was a respect that lasted until his death; some part may have been because of her status as a Rani Sahiba, but some

Naina Devi practising with her harmonium

part was based on a familial feeling on both sides and a fatherly instinct on his part. He realized, perhaps, that here was one who had transcended the social disapproval of her chosen genre, and dedicated herself to its beauty, its femininity, its musical heritage, and who had intuitively voiced its innate truths, all as a matter of courageous choice.

Theirs was an extraordinary collaboration. In the world of music he was an aristocrat from a lineage of extraordinary distinction, the famed Rampur-Sahaswan gharana, and his family tree blossomed with musicians of very high calibre. The gharana's origin began with Ustad Mehboob Khan who was a khayal singer at the royal court of the Nawab of Rampur; his musical tradition was continued by his son, Ustad Inayat Hussain Khan—who is considered the actual founder of the gharana—and by his sons-in-law, one of whom was Mushtaq Hussain Khan. It was all very interconnected and within the family, as it were, and the name Sahaswan came from their ancestral home in the district of Badaun.

The gharana was prolific in its talent, both in terms of performers from within the family as well as those who learned from them, and for close to a century has enriched the scene of Hindustani music with artistes like Ustad Nissar Hussain Khan and his star pupil Ustad Rashid Khan of contemporary times; Ustad Ghulam Sadiq Khan, Ustad Hafeez Ahmed Khan, Ustad Sarfaraz Hussain Khan, Ustad Ghulam Mustafa Khan and others too numerous to name. Mushtaq Hussain Khan's own list of pupils from outside the family was a stellar one: it included Vidushi Shanno Khurana, Vidushi Sulochana Brahaspati, Vidushi Sumati Mutatkar and his own nephew, the brilliant qawwal, Ustad Jafar Hussain Khan.

Mushtaq Hussain Khan was a musician even before he was born, goes the legend, and it is true that his training began when he was just a child. His father-in-law was his chief mentor, his guide and his guru. Sometimes he practiced for more than 16 hours a day, so immersed in the experience that he would float into a trance. His extraordinary talent earned him the position of one of the court musicians in Rampur, then he was elevated to

Chief Court Musician. Very soon, he was a regular at music conferences across the country and recognized as an outstanding exponent of the arts. In 1956, when he was in his late 70s, he retired from Rampur and joined the Kendra the following year. He was awarded the Padma Bhushan in 1957, amongst the first Hindustani singers to receive this honour.

After his death in 1964, Naina Devi wrote a monograph on her revered Ustad which was published by the Sangeet Natak Akademi. In that short time as his pupil she had learned much from him and formed bonds with him.

It was to him that she owed her introduction to the Dargah in Bareilly, the Khanqah-e-Niazia visited by many musicians, and to its revered Pir, Hazrat Shah Mohammed Taqi, also known as Aziz Miyan, in whom the Ustad had implicit faith; and like him Naina Devi became a devotee of Aziz Miyan.

The Khanqah had a venerable history, being founded in 1776 by Maulvi Shah Niaz Ahmed, a Sufi poet and mystic who was born to a deeply spiritual family in Delhi, where he attended a madrasa of which he later became the principal. It was Hazrat Maulana Fakhar-e-Jahan, his spiritual mentor, who sent Niaz to Bareilly where he established the Sufi order known as the Niazia Silsila. He was also a literary figure, as so many Sufi saints were: through their writings and poetry they sought to act as a bridge between the human and the divine. Apart from the scholarly books he wrote on aspects of theology, he wrote poetry which still touches us with its imagery and echoes of yearning, and the deft turns of phrase that can be interpreted—as they are meant to be—in more than one way, worldly or spiritual:

The moment You unveiled Your face to display Your splendour,
It was the very moment You turned me into a mirror.

and

I met you by chance, walking down the pathways of life,
and my heart could never remain still after that.

More than two centuries later, following generations of successors, was born the little boy who would become Aziz Miyan, the Sajjada Nashin who would carry forward the Niazia Silsila, a task he willingly accepted and undertook for 44 years until his death in 1968. He brought his many talents to bear on his spiritual and human duties, and while he was an accomplished hunter, horseman and calligrapher, he was known for his generosity and compassion to the needy. He fed the poor, and bore the expenses for the weddings of their daughters and made sure that free medicines were distributed to them. Of course, he wrote: learned tomes as well as poetry in Urdu, Hindi and Persian, and he was an orator whose message echoed the Sufi refrain of *Sulh-e-Kul*, or Peace to All, reflecting on the messages of all faiths, that the Divine is present in all of us.

But most of all, he had a very sensitive ear for music and composed a special *qaul* and qawwalis for the Khanqah. This empathy for music created an atmosphere that was especially attractive to musicians and dancers, many of whom flocked to the Dargah to become his disciples, Hindus as well as Muslims, the best of the best: Ustad Ahmad Jan Thirakwa, Ustad Mushtaq Hussain Khan, Pandit Birju Maharaj, and his uncles, Pandit Lachchu Maharaj and Pandit Shambhu Maharaj, Pandit V.G. Jog, Uma Sharma, the Dagar brothers, Ustad Nasir Hussain and Ustad Zaheeruddin Dagar and Naina Devi.

But there is a story behind their first meeting. She had suddenly lost her voice, for a singer the worst possible nightmare. It came at a time when she had begun to perform and was getting to be known. Frantically she went from doctor to doctor but none of their medicines seemed to work. Finally it was her Ustad who guided her: 'You must go to the Pir of Bareilly, he is the only one who can help you.' There again, fate did not seem to be on her side as her first attempts did not lead to a meeting. Eventually it was when Ustad Mushtaq Hussain Khan took her to Bareilly, that she was able to meet Aziz Miyan; the Pir simply touched her throat and told her that all would be well. He said: 'From this moment, all your worries are mine. Go in peace; everything will be all right.'

Vidya Rao, Naina Devi's student, describes her response in the biography that she wrote: *Heart to Heart: Remembering Nainaji*:

> I felt a sense of great peace, of relief, as if someone had lifted a huge load off my head. I knew with an extraordinary certainty, that nothing and no one could ever harm me. I was safe, and more than safe, alive in a way that I had not experienced before. When I left, Pir Sahib blessed me and said, '*Ustad se lo taleem, mujhse taseer*' (learn the techniques of music, its intricacies from your ustad, but the essence of music, its secret heart, take that from me)...
>
> I returned to Delhi. I was cured, singing again, and with his blessings, better than ever before. Truly, Pir Sahib had given me the elusive gift of *taseer*. This is not something that can be learnt or acquired through *riyaz*. It just has to be, to come spontaneously, like a blessing, like divine grace.

There are many ways to describe *taseer*: some say it is the feeling that wells out from the performer's music to form a strong and intangible bond with the listener; the connect that unites, that inspires and moves; one that does not depend only on high technical accomplishment but is transcendental and works on a mystical plane. Taseer implies also an element of surrender, an almost spiritual intervention, which affects both performer and audience to create a profound musical experience. Naina Devi understood its power and ascribed her abilities as performer, teacher, student and composer to this gift and to the blessings of Aziz Miyan.

This was the beginning of the very deep bond that she shared with the Dargah and the Pir, and of her annual *Urs* pilgrimages to Bareilly and to Ajmer, to the shrine of Khwaja Garib Nawaz. The feeling of safety made the Dargah a place of refuge where, even if for the moment, her troubles or worries could be set aside; and the connections with music and musicians gave it a feeling of homecoming. It was a spiritual anchor for her, a respite from the world, a place where she belonged wholly and beyond question. By this time in her life she had been through much: she had borne it uncomplainingly and with courage, always showing a brave face; but deep down, there must have been moments of loneliness despite the camaraderie of the *mehfils* in Delhi

and the friendship of musicians. An ache, perhaps, for her own family so far away, the only people to whom she could open up and with whom she could share confidences. In the end, it was her association with the Khanqah-e-Niazi that healed and nourished her.

And such was her feeling of belonging that she, unused to asking for anything for herself, once sought material help from the Pir. It was 1965 and the wedding of her son Ratanjit was about to take place. The invitations were being sent, as was the custom, in the name of his grandfather Raja Charanjit Singh; but there was simply no money nor could she ask her father-in-law. Clearly, the invitees would have some expectations of how this aristocratic wedding would be conducted, but how was she to fulfill this? Her younger son Karanjit accompanied her to Bareilly; she wept as she sat at the feet of her Pir. 'How is this wedding going to happen, where will the money come from, the cards have gone under Raja sahib's name and it's a matter of his honour…' Aziz Miyan told her not to worry and gave her Rs 10,000

Ratanjit's wedding reception in Delhi; the groom and his bride, Pronoti (nee Barooah), with Raja sahib on the left

for the wedding, a sum that tided her through this crisis. It is not recorded whether Raja sahib himself expressed any concern for the finances of his grandson's wedding.

Like other artistes who came to the Dargah, she too paid her homage through musical offerings at the shrine in the presence of the devout and of the Pir. Many musicians (the late Ustad Jafar Hussain Khan among them) have spoken of how, on such occasions, they performed almost as if in a trance: the 'self' and the space around them dissolved into nothingness, leaving only the humble pilgrim and the music he offered in a state of complete surrender. Their utter belief in the shrine and its Pir was a magnet that brought them back time and again.

Quite possibly this attachment was also the beginning of her involvement with Sufism and her studies of its concepts. Maybe it reminded her of childhood in Bengal with its echoes of Lallan Faqir and of the Baul singers. Perhaps it was the embedded memory of her grandfather and his open-hearted universalism. In his *Shlokasangraha*, the book of devotional lessons, the title page bore the inscription 'The Wide Universe is the Temple of God', while within were included excerpts from the great scriptures of Hinduism, Christianity, Islam, and other faiths. In the same way, there was something very inclusive about the Dargah, it cut across the barriers of religion and was a symbol of the syncretic tradition of India. For generations its pirs had stressed humanity and universal brotherhood and they counted many non-Muslims amongst their disciples.

Many of her projects, and her exploration of ideas in her writings, reflected this increasing fascination for syncretic philosophies, and one of her papers, 'Integration, a Heritage of the Performing Arts', written in 1987, is reproduced at the end of this book as an example. It was reflected also, in a very personal way, in her puja space where the picture of her Pir rested alongside images of the Devi and Krishna.

But this thinking (and perhaps her attachment to the Dargah) also caused people to be deeply critical of her. She was viewed as a person who only

liked Muslim musicians; in fact, was so pro-Muslim that she would only promote Muslim musicians to the detriment of others. Her lifestyle was seen as not being in consonance with that of a Hindu woman or even that of a royal lady. However, this is something of an overstatement. The fact is that she was the disciple of Ustad Mushtaq Hussain Khan, a member of a large family of musicians who all tended to be rather clannish, unsurprising since the weight of an entire gharana rested on their collective shoulders. In that closeness to their families she had clearly imbibed many of their traditions and observances which she was happy to share with them. But for her, music was music, talent was talent; and eventually this could be viewed as just a stick with which to beat her.

Kathak

One of the most singular achievements of the Bharatiya Kala Kendra was the revival of the Kathak dance form in Delhi; at that time, Kathak was virtually unknown. Two of the major gharanas—Lucknow and Jaipur—were represented by Guru Shambhu Maharaj and Guru Sundar Prasad respectively, and the students learnt from both masters. They worked hard together to take the tradition forward. It was Nirmala Joshi who invited Birju Maharaj to join his uncle at the Kendra, and his primary task was not only that of assistance in teaching but also to undertake the choreography of small items, ballets and dance dramas. But there was a paucity of trained dancers in Delhi; the first ballet included Sumitra Charat Ram's family members; when the first Ram Leela was staged in 1957 her two daughters and other children came onstage to act as monkeys. Dancers had to be brought in from Bengal, but slowly, the corps was built up, and so was its repertoire. Dance dramas like *Malti Madhav*, *Kumar Sambhav* and *Shaan-e-Awadh* were staged for responsive audiences.

Naina Devi was involved on a day-to-day basis, looking after and at the dancers, absorbing all the techniques and processes of the back-of-the-house and onstage preparations. Her learning experience embraced not just the form—she was already familiar with it—but also the study of its individual movements and its physical enactments of narratives and the spoken word.

Naina Devi with Kathak maestro Birju Maharaj (left) and dancer Roshan Kumari (right)

She always enjoyed the experience of '*bhav batana*' where a seated dancer would skillfully use face, eyes and hands to communicate the emotion and depth of poetry. *Shaan-e-Awadh* reminded her of the very close relations between *thumri* and Kathak, especially as expressed in the grand court of Nawab Wajid Ali Shah.

The dance dramas also engaged her aesthetic sense and her innate feeling for presentation. She took an interest in many different aspects: costumes and colours, stage and sets, even lighting. Tapas Sen, the lighting master who used to come from Calcutta especially for the Kendra's presentation of the *Ram Leela*, was a person with whom she would have long discussions in Bengali on lights, how they could be used, the nuances of usage...It must have taken her right back to her days in Calcutta with her *mejdi*, Sadhona, with *Ali Baba* and the highly professional stage direction of Modhu Bose.

A major production was the dance drama *Kumar Sambhav* based on the work by Kalidasa. One of its high points was the duet between Birju Maharaj and Kumudini Lakhia as Kamdev and Rati respectively. It was Naina Devi who

designed the costumes and supervised the coordination for this landmark production. And that continued through the years; she helped dancers like Uma Sharma and Shovana Narayan with their costumes, even helping in choosing the materials and jewellery. She guided them in concepts of restraint, not overdoing embellishments or colours; in gauging the difference between a TV presentation and a live performance, and helping them understand that every medium has its own demands. And then there was the travel: with a large dance group from the Kendra to the former Soviet Union, with another group to the United States and later, within India criss-crossing the country by third-class train with large entourages of singers and dancers, all of whom ate railway food together and felt like a part of one big family.

Rampur

There are some patterns that weave themselves across our lives and we never really recognize them until much later. Rampur was like a recurring melodic phrase, a place and state of mind that Naina Devi returned to literally and metaphorically. But her very first brush with Rampur was in the mid-1920s when she was a little child, and while it has been written about already, it bears repetition as a story of singular determination, one which foreshadows some aspects of Naina Devi's later life: and yet there is an impish charm to the tale.

She was then only eight years old and her parents were invited to Emerald Bower, the home of Raja Prodyut Kumar Tagore, for a reception in honour of the Nawab and Begum of Rampur at which the Viceroy and Vicereine would also be present. Because she knew that after the banquet there would be a '*naach*' (or '*nautch*' as it used to be called), a song and dance performance by *tawaifs*, she wanted to go and begged and pleaded with her parents to take her. They in turn must have been quite taken aback at the idea of taking a small child to such an unsuitable occasion—where, moreover, she was not even invited—they refused, but eventually could not hold out against the entreaties of little Nilina. The child had come up with a plan to circumvent both protocol and objection: she could stay with the Begum in her room at Emerald Bower (the Begum being in purdah) and could watch from behind the ornamental grills that screened the privacy of the zenana. Nobody, except for the Begum, would even know that she was present. With this assurance her parents allowed her, however reluctantly, to accompany them.

How her eyes must have widened as the *naach* commenced. Here were the most famous tawaifs of Calcutta gathered together in one place for a performance: perhaps she would never see another such gathering of brilliance in her life. But at the age of eight, how aware was she of what she was looking at, or who these women were? Did she even know what a *tawaif* meant? Certainly she enjoyed what must have been a night of spectacular dance and music, for she remembered those performers and their performances throughout her life and was able to recall them in detail. The memory of that night went beyond mere enjoyment; maybe it was at that moment that a deep and intangible bond with the figure and the idea of the *tawaif* began to shape in her mind. That particular night, though, was all about the galaxy of stars in front of her.

Gauhar Jaan

There was Gauhar Jaan, the reigning courtesan, a celebrity of such fame that her picture appeared on matchbox labels; a recording star whose discs uncovered her amazing range, not only in the genres she sang so fluidly but also languages, for she sang in Arabic, Tamil and Pashto. So well-known and popular was she that she was—despite all social disapproval—selected to perform at the imperial Delhi Durbar of 1911, and was able to command the highest of fees for her appearances. At the same time, she was acknowledged as a classical music artiste of high standing by none other than the music scholar and connoisseur, Vishnu Narayan Bhatkhande.

Then there was Jaddan Bai, pupil of Ustad Moizuddin Khan himself, whose other distinguished teacher was Ustad Barkat Ali Khan. She had a little daughter affectionately called Baby Rani; later, mother and child moved

Jaddan Bai

to Bombay (now Mumbai) and the world would flock to theatres to see the daughter, now known as Nargis and a major film star in her own right.

And there was Janaki Bai Allahabadi, also known as Chhappan Chhuriwali. A jealous lover is said to have scarred her face with 56 knife strokes, hence the name. Nonetheless— her beauty marred forever—she was a very popular singer whose talent had been honed by Ustad Hassu Khan of the Gwalior Gharana. She wrote verse and composed music; and she too was a major recording star whose discs sold in vast numbers.

That night in Emerald Bower two links were forged that would impact the whole of Nilina's life. The first was her enduring fascination for the persona of the *tawaif*; and the second, her friendship with the elegant young Begum of Rampur, Princess Rafat Zamani, who had been so kind to her that evening.

The city of Rampur lay on the tripartite axis of high culture that joined the Imperial Mughal court of Delhi with that of Awadh. Like the other two cities, it had poetry; and such an abundance of great musicians and music that the city had its own gharana; there was also a distinctive cuisine featuring dishes like Rampuri fish, Rampuri korma, and *adrak ka halwa*. In the heyday of that royal kitchen, individual chefs had their own specialities: if one was an expert in *shab degh*, then the other was the master of desserts such as *dar behest* and *habshi halwa*.

But Rampur had assets that the other two cities did not. It had (and still has) what is possibly the largest and finest library of Islamic manuscripts, paintings and calligraphy specimens in Asia. The origins date back to the 18th century and the personal collection of Nawab Faizullah Khan. His descendants, most of them patrons of scholars, poets and painters, added to this peerless treasure trove, which now comprises thousands of manuscripts, books and examples of calligraphy. There are printed works in Sanskrit and Hindi; there are works of great rarity such as a seventh century Quran written on parchment; a Persian translation of Valmiki's *Ramayana*; and an illustrated manuscript which is the Persian translation of the Panchatantra fables with beautiful paintings depicting the stories.

And the other asset: Rampur had the Rampur Hound, its native breed of dog created by Nawab Ahmad Ali Khan by combining the bloodlines of the Afghan Tazi and the British greyhound. The result was an animal that matched great endurance with amazing speed, which made it a favoured hound for hunting. Unfortunately, as hunting declined so did the demand for the dog: today, like other Indian breeds, the Rampur Hound is dying out.

As Rani Nina Ripjit Singh, she had the opportunity to visit Rampur when the family crossed the northern Indian plains between Awadh and Delhi on their winter visits to Rajanagar and Shahjahanpur. They were the guests of the Nawab at the Khasbagh Palace; Nina may have been able to listen to music here, as Nawab Raza Ali Khan was a patron and connoisseur whose court muscians were superb artistes and who himself played the khartaal. She was always warmly welcomed by Begum Rafat Zamani of Rampur. Photographs of the Begum usually show her at her elegant best clad in traditional garments: brocaded *farshi* pyjamas embellished with *karchobi*

embroidery, a silk chiffon kameez and a long six yard chiffon *odhni* with elaborate borders draped over her head and trailing almost to the floor.

Begum Rafat Zamani of Rampur

Many years later, the connections with Rampur would multiply. As Naina Devi, Nina would become the pupil of Ustad Mushtaq Hussain Khan, maestro of the Rampur-Sahaswan gharana, when he came to Delhi. And the Begum would become one of the first Patrons of Raag Rang, an organization for the promotion of music and the performing arts instituted by Naina Devi in 1962.

Raag Rang 1

Naina Devi's experience at the Bharatiya Kala Kendra had been the making of her in so many ways. It was as if having been rejected by one family she came into the open arms of another: the deep friendship with Sumitra Charat Ram, with Nirmala Joshi, with Sharda Rao, was a balm that restored her confidence and served as the reassuring foundation for a new life; her daily contact with music and dance, with all the creative artistes who wandered in and out of her home, encouraged her to be a performer in her own right. She had entered a freer, more open world. A liberating world. A new world. Not the world of Nilina, not the world of Rani Nina Ripjit Singh. It was the world of Naina Devi.

And here she had tasted the freedom of artistic creativity within a supporting structure. Now she was ready to enter a new phase of her artistic life by creating a structure of her own, the institution of Raag Rang. But while she formally exited from the Bharatiya Kala Kendra, she kept alive all those ties that meant so much to her. The friendship with Sumitra Charat Ram continued; no family occasion was complete without Naina Devi's presence;

very often, her advice or opinion was sought and the discussions would continue long into the night.

In many ways Raag Rang was an embodiment of her deeply-held belief in the syncretic culture of India. The title itself was an indication: she felt that the grammar of 'Raag' was rooted in the ancient textual traditions of Sanskrit, whereas 'Rang' came with the advent of the Muslims, especially the Sufis, and represented their contribution to Hindustani music. She invited the well-known artist, M.F. Hussain, to design the logo and he followed her idea by presenting the word Raag in a sort of Devnagari style and the word Rang more like Urdu. It was an interesting concept, and though some did not agree with this interpretation, all its supporters were in agreement with its objectives: 'to propagate the traditional arts of music and dance to create an atmosphere of music and widen the awareness of this aspect of our culture.'

Naina Devi had been a shrewd observer of the growth of the Bharatiya Kala Kendra. She realized that it was easy enough to establish an institution in the first flush of enthusiasm; what was more difficult and very essential was to sustain it over time without a flagging of interest. She saw that three things at least were necessary: a core of superb performing talent to present to audiences; the creative spark for programming that would catch interest and be educative as well as enjoyable; and importantly, the financing, without which ideas could not be implemented. Besides this, the support of friends and fellow connoisseurs—not forgetting the artistes themselves—was much needed. And, in a city like Delhi, it always helped to maintain contacts with official quarters.

The people she asked to join her organization in different capacities reflected the balance she sought. There were musicians and musical experts, there were important and influential people, there were people who could help to bring in finances, there were those whose names added lustre to any panel and then there were those who simply enjoyed music and supported her vision wholeheartedly.

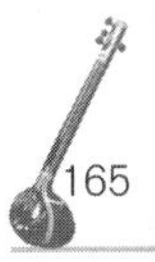

A Raag Rang brochure records the names of those involved: the Patrons included not only the Begum of Rampur (listed as the Rajmata Sahiba of Rampur) but also the Maharani of Nabha and the hotel magnate Rai Bahadur M.S. Oberoi. The list of Founders included Ustad Bade Ghulam Ali Khan, Ustad Vilayat Khan and her guru-bhai Sunil Bose, as also Keshav Kothari, a former student of Shambhu Maharaj, whose cultural expertise enabled him to later become the Secretary of the Sangeet Natak Akademi. And the list of artiste members went beyond the traditional scope of musicians and dancers—such as Ustad Bismillah Khan, Rasoolan Bai, Begum Akhtar and Girija Devi—to include others, people from the world of art such as M.F. Hussain and noted poet and art critic Keshav Malik; people from media, such as Jai Chandiram from Doordarshan; and people connected with the government. The list was not static. It grew with Raag Rang itself, and the list for 1970 includes the then Lt Governor of Delhi, Dr A.N. Jha as a Patron along with Maharaja Yadvendra Singh of Patiala; and Anjani Bai Malpekar as a member.

An informal music session at home with the famed singer Anjani Bai Malpekar (seated)

Naina Devi and Siddheshwari Devi exchanging smiles and views before a concert

Some of the Raag Rang events were elaborately planned, where music and dance were accompanied by seminars and discussions which drew in other disciplines. Some had a more light-hearted and spontaneous approach. One occasion which has remained an indelible memory for the people who were present took place not in a hall or room but on the banks of the Yamuna river at Okhla. On a night illuminated by the brilliant light of the moon it celebrated Gulabi Chaiti with the music of that languorous season, the forerunner of the heat of summer. What made it extraordinary was the presence of a large number of musicians in that one place at the same time. Almost all the great divas were there: Siddheshwari Devi, Rasoolan Bai, Begum Akhtar, Girija Devi, as well as Bade Ghulam Ali Khan, the Dagars and Ram Chatur Malik. What made it even more extraordinary was the way that this mehfil became a shared musical experience of give-and-take between the artistes. After a number of solo performances, they sang a *chaiti*. It began with a single line which one of them sang, this was picked up by the

The three divas of *thumri*: Siddheshwari Devi, Badi Moti Bai and Rasoolan Bai

others, one by one, each of whom sang the line each time improvising on it in different ways to show fresh musical possibilities. This game of melodies was linked like some beautiful chain. From it emerged some wonderful music as the artistes inspired each other and learned from each other in a cordial atmosphere of respect and affection. It is difficult to imagine that such a thing could happen today: much of it was because of Naina Devi's ability to bring musicians together and bind them as family, her enveloping sense of a musical '*biradari*', as Shubha Mudgal, her student, describes it.

In 1965, when Mrs Indira Gandhi was the Minister for Information and Broadcasting, Naina Devi was asked to work on performing arts programmes for All India Radio and later Doordarshan, then the only TV channel in the country. It was a job tailor-made for her, giving her ample opportunity to exercise her creative imagination and share her vast knowledge of music with a much wider audience. She worked on this side by side with her work for Raag Rang which was ongoing and intensely active. But she conceived and executed some brilliant programmes, such as her interviews with many renowned musicians including her guru bhai, the tabla genius Ustad Ahmed

Jan Thirakwa, Pandit Bhimsen Joshi and many others. In one television series she gave a vivid description of the history of Hindustani music by setting its principal genres in the courts where they were nurtured: *dhrupad* in Gwalior, khayal in Delhi at the Mughal court of Mohammed Shah Rangila and her beloved *thumri* at the Awadhi court of Nawab Wajid Ali Shah. This gave her ample opportunity to highlight the costumes and manners of the times and create a riveting picture of those eras through music and dance.

Of course she highlighted her favourite topic, the *thumri*, with yet another programme: *Tarikh-e-Thumri* which brought together great exponents of the form, Badi Moti Bai, Rasoolan Bai and Siddheshwari Devi. She herself had learnt the intricacies of the Purab Ang of the *thumri* from Rasoolan Bai, a master of the form, and always gave her the respect due to a guru. Indeed, there was so much activity in her life that her personal situation became quite secondary. Yet soon enough it would come to the fore again.

Raja Charanjit Singh

As a teenager, Reggie had found it galling to see how shabbily his mother had been treated by his grandfather. But with him, as with all her children, Naina Devi insisted that not only should the relationship be maintained, but that there should be no bitterness. By the mid-1960s, her daughters and sons were no longer children, they were young adults who had found their own paths in life. She herself had gone well beyond her shock and hurt at the treatment she had received. Her life was overflowing with all the activities she was engaged in, all the friends she had made, and her music: her own performances and the many *mehfils* she held as well as attended. There was really no time for dwelling on the past because there was so much to do in the present. Besides which her present, so happy, so fulfilling, had been made possible only by that past which had cast her out of her husband's family. Perhaps, rather than bitterness, she should feel thankful for all the things that had happened and all the opportunities that followed.

Her contact with Raja Charanjit Singh had resumed on a sporadic basis. There were unintentional comic moments; once, while she was still singing

incognito and he remained completely unaware of it, she was practising with Ustad Ghulam Sabir Khan, the renowned sarangi player who was then her teacher, when suddenly there was a hubbub outside. Someone said 'Sarkar is coming!' With remarkable speed and suppleness the sarangi maestro (who was large of size with a well-built body) made an exit by leaping through an open window, leaving no trace of his presence behind.

But at some point, Raja Charanjit Singh must have felt the gaping vacuum in his own life. The world had changed and he was getting older. His grandchildren were no longer obliged to spend holidays with him. When loneliness and ageing come together it is a terrible thing, a bleakness of the soul. Slowly his barriers started to fall. When June (Nilika), who was then a young widow, thought of re-marrying, he was not at all pleased because the rigid traditionalist in him came to the fore. It was in that context that he remembered Naina Devi. In the ample gardens of his Bareilly house, as he and Kenny were sipping coffee together, he remarked, 'You know, Kenny, Nina really loved Rip, she chose not to marry anyone else.' It was said with a degree of approval.

LEFT Surrounded by bridesmaids, Nilika (June) awaits her wedding ceremony
RIGHT June and her bridegroom during the Anand Karaj. She is supported by her uncle, Raja Padamjit Singh

Of course, there came a time when he became aware of her connection with music and the fact that she was singing in public. He did not like it very much, but it was a different world now; women from respected families were becoming singers and dancers, and the connotation of their performances had changed from common entertainment to culture and art. He appreciated the fact that she had respected his feelings and those of the family by adopting a pseudonym for her musical persona. Even so, in the earlier years Naina Devi must have worried a little about how he would respond to her chosen life; but she soon got over it; she had to because she had to carry on with what she had started. He came to Delhi for a cataract operation and she dutifully visited him as he recuperated. He came to their house on Birbal Road; and each time he came to Delhi, Naina Devi would make it a point to meet him and so the relationship continued.

Slowly everybody became accustomed to the new regime; and when Raja Charanjit Singh began visiting them it was clear that he had accepted her way of life. So much so that she actually arranged a musical performance by Ustad Jafar Hussain Khan in their Jangpura home to which he came. And perhaps that was the moment when he accepted that yes, she was now Naina Devi, and belonged to the world of music. That acceptance was the only apology he could make for those lost years.

It took a long time for Reggie to make peace with his grandfather, the wound was deep. When finally he saw him as a vulnerable and broken old man before he passed away in 1970, that was the moment he was able to perceive things differently and with compassion.

For some time Raja sahib had been under the care of his daughter, Pamela, in nearby Shahjahanpur, but the situation became difficult for her. Nor could she come to Bareilly for any length of time because she was recently widowed and had her own home and children to look after. Matters now came to a stage where she could no longer deal with them; Pamela, in desperation, broke her long silence and turned to her sister-in-law to say, 'Now you better come and take over, because I can't handle him anymore.'

And Raja sahib himself sent a pathos-filled note to her, 'Nina, I need you.' The very dependence and helplessness of its tone was so unlike him that she realized immediate action was needed.

Raja Charanjit Singh was brought back to Chapslee in the summer of 1970. It was during the searing days of high summer when Naina Devi, accompanied by Kenny and Reggie's young daughter, Potli, went to Bareilly to fetch him. Her first sight of him shocked her, so pale and weak and somehow unkempt and uncared for. His feet were bare and they were dirty. She asked for a basin of water and put his feet in it to soak. 'What are you doing?' he asked. She replied, 'I want to clean your feet.' He was a man who never showed his feelings, yet in that moment (and, who knows, perhaps for the first time in his adult life) his eyes were moist. The railway station at Bareilly was like a furnace as they boarded the train with a huge amount of baggage on that final trip to Simla. But after arriving in Simla, he had a stroke and lapsed into a coma for two months.

It was a very difficult time for Naina Devi because Reggie's wife was in an advanced stage of pregnancy and they were rotating between Simla and the plains. She herself had to stay in Simla to organize minor structural changes to the ground floor at Chapslee, to cater to medical needs including day and night nursing, and all the equipment. Kenny stayed with her, but Raja sahib was now beyond help, and finally in August he slipped away forever. Surely she must have felt sadness; such a close association begun more than 30 years ago severed forever; such a life of needless loneliness, what a waste! But she did not allow bitterness to cloud her mourning, not then or ever, choosing to maintain silence about what had happened after her husband died.

Raag Rang 2

Just over 10 years after she started Raag Rang, Naina Devi had cause to look back with quiet satisfaction. The organization was still active and a lot had been accomplished despite a constant funds crunch. The list of artistes who had performed at formal concerts and informal *mehfils* was long and distinguished; it included legendary musicians like Ustad Bismillah Khan, Pandit Ravi Shankar, Vidushi Gangubai Hangal, Ustad Ahmed Jan Thirakwa, Pandit Radha Mohan Moitra, and Kumar Gandharva, to name only a few. Raag Rang had presented Badi Moti Bai of Benaras, the only surviving disciple of the great Moizuddin Khan, for the first time in Delhi. Her performance of *thumris* was rapturously acclaimed by the critics: '...sung in an intensely lyrical vein and alive with exquisite shades of colouring...as emotionally appealing as it was musically seductive...'

Her contribution to the cause of the performing arts and music in particular brought her public recognition through the award of the Padma Shri in 1974. This spurred her on to the creation of more programmes; she celebrated the seasons with music and dance, first the rains of the monsoon with Sawan Bhadon, then the fresh young days of spring with Rang Basanti.

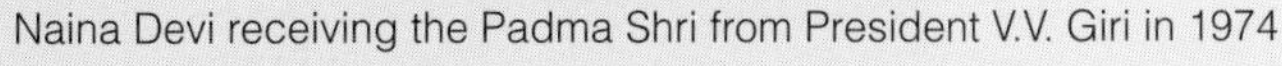

Naina Devi receiving the Padma Shri from President V.V. Giri in 1974

For her ambitious six-day festival and symposium titled Bansuri, she enlisted the support of other organisations, the Sangeet Natak Akademi and the Sahitya Kala Parishad. Here she returned to her favourite theme of the syncretic nature of Northern Indian performing arts and she featured different forms of music and dance which evolved and developed through the influence of the Vaishnavite and Sufi traditions whose approach was very similar. Her metaphor was the flute: the flute of Krishna and of Rumi whose haunting refrains of love and separation echoed the yearning of the soul for sublimation. The performing arts she chose to feature included a wide range, from Baul, Haveli Sangeet and qawwali to the music of the flute, the sarod, sitar and santoor, and to dance forms like Odissi and Manipuri and—of course—Kathak. The accompanying symposium had distinguished panels with moderators such as Prof Nurul Hasan, Justice Rangaraj and Dr Kapila Vatsyayan guiding discussions on topics such as 'Sufism in Punjab' and the 'Traditions of Brindaban'.

With Prime Minister Indira Gandhi and the LP of the music of Sawan Bhadon, ca 1981

Naina Devi presents eminent qawwals, the Sabri Brothers from Pakistan, with a memento from Raag Rang

Quite apart from the programmes for Raag Rang, a deep concern for artistes and their well-being was always on her mind. She had seen for herself how a twist of fate could send fortunes plummeting and endanger livelihoods. After Rasoolan Bai's house was burnt down during communal riots in Ahmedabad, she invited the homeless singer to come to Delhi and stay with her; and she came, along with the entire family whose only support she was, some 13 people in number. For some time, they were looked after by Naina Devi. When Rasoolan Bai needed medical assistance after a paralytic stroke, it was Raag Rang which funded the initial expenses for her hospital treatment. Many other measures were initiated by Naina Devi, including medical insurance for artistes and scholarships obtained through the Ministry of Education for needy students of music or dance.

She had also envisaged establishing an Artistes' Centre, to be called Aditya Bhavan, in Delhi. It was to be a multi-purpose centre, a place for teaching the music of the traditional gharanas, where old and needy artistes could be housed and visiting artistes provided hostel accommodation. The plans included a library for music, films and books. Though the foundation stone of the Centre was laid in 1968, unfortunately the project came to naught with a change of officials. What did succeed, however, was an Artiste's Colony in New Delhi in an area where a new block of apartments was being constructed. The initial idea came from dancer Uma Sharma who suggested it to the then Lt Governor of Delhi, Dr A.N. Jha, and got him to sign an order for allotments. But the follow-up was undertaken by Naina Devi as Uma was going away for six months. We can only imagine the wearisome process of the follow-up and the many visits to government offices: but at last the quota for musicians and artistes came and many artistes were able to buy accommodation and with it, peace of mind.

Her informal *mehfils* at home were legendary in the world of music. Nobody was ever sure who would be present or would simply decide to drop in at the last moment. But everybody knew that each would be warmly welcomed and that the evening would flow with music and stories and—who knows—perhaps impromptu recitals by maestros. On one such evening, Ustad Ahmed Jan Thirakwa began singing a *thumri* in raag Piloo and was joined by the likes of Ustad Amir Khan, Ustad Yunus Hussain Khan and Pandit Debu Chaudhuri, Pandit Samta Prasad and Naina Devi herself. What an evening that must have been!

Famed Pakistani artiste, Roshana Begum (centre), flanked by Naina Devi (left) and Dipali Nag (right). Also in the picture is Uma Vasudev (top left) between dance critic Sunil Kothari and singer Ustad Munawar Ali Khan. The singer Malati Gilani is seated near Naina Devi

She was always keenly aware of how much talent languished on the sidelines for lack of attention or promotion; and she was tireless in promoting all such artistes . One of them was the singer, Ustad Jafar Hussain Khan of Badaun, whose mellow rendition of qawwali was tempered by the fine nuances of the Rampur gharana. Once Vinod Kapur, an ardent music lover, had engaged a singer for a pre-wedding soiree, designed as a family occasion with a predominantly younger audience in full celebration mode. The singer was a comely lady whose flirtatious airs and chirpy but suggestive lyrics were suited for just such an evening; but with barely two days to go, she cancelled the concert which had been booked two months in advance, pleading a contractual clash. Now what to do? He turned to Naina Devi for help; she suggested Jafar Hussain Khan. A qawwali singer was emphatically not what he was looking for, still less a male singer. He was dubious, she was reassuring. 'Don't worry,' she told him, 'Jafar sings wonderfully. He will manage your audience with his repertoire. In any case, at this point we have no choice!'

That was indeed the truth…but when Jafar began singing, the magic of his voice took over and the audience was entranced. Like Oliver Twist, they demanded more; this one concert opened many doors for the musician and requests for many other singing appointments.

As the decade of the 1980s advanced, the very last brochure issued by Raag Rang in 1986 celebrated the Silver Jubilee of the organisation. Very possibly that was also its last major event. Twenty-five years: a whole quarter century had gone by, almost as if in a flash. When she thought of the past, her life in music actually spanned more than 60 years, dating back to when she was just a child sitting at the feet of Girija Babu. And how many things had changed since then; it was a different music now in the way that it was taught, in its ambience and presentation; in the way that it was listened to. The mass popularity of film music across the country had impacted certain genres, on the other hand, since much was borrowed from folk music and classical raag, at least the melodies still resonated with large swathes of people. (This was, of course, before the time of rock and fusion).

Seen in *jugalbandi*, Ustad Bismillah Khan and Naina Devi at the Raag Rang Silver Jubilee, 1986. Her student Vidya Rao gives support on the tanpura

The Silver Jubilee celebrations included three evenings of stellar performances, among them a *jugalbandi* between Ustad Bismillah Khan and Naina Devi, also featuring dancers Uma Sharma and Ram Mohan, and singers Munawwar Ali Khan, Ustad Jafar Hussain Khan and Shipra Bose. And, most fittingly, the incomparable Girija Devi, who had been the artiste of the evening all those years ago at Raag Rang's inaugural *mehfil* in 1962, also sang at this celebration 25 years later.

Last Years

Sometimes when you are focused on a single point agenda, it is all you can see, all you can feel, you revolve around it like a spinning top quite oblivious to the rest of the world whirling around you. It is a metaphor you could aptly use for those who bring a singular intensity and focus to what they do, and in many ways it describes Naina Devi's later life which had been quite taken over by her musical activities, in fact, her life *was* her musical activities. This is not to say that it was a grim life: on the contrary, it was filled with joy and with her silvery laughter and with the sheer pleasure of singing, or being with fellow artistes, or teaching, or planning some new programme for Raag Rang. Now it was Raag Rang that filled her mind and occupied her hours. But in a sense it was so utterly sufficient for her and so absorbing that certain other aspects of socialization simply disappeared.

In the last years of her life it was her grandson, Chandrajit, lovingly called Baba, who stayed with her as a college student from the time he was 18 years old and became her friend and companion. He had a natural affinity for classical music, much enhanced by a rich listening experience both in her home and at the *mehfils* that he occasionally went to with her. On her summer visits to Chapslee she used to practise at home and record for the Simla station of AIR. Although Baba learnt from her briefly, it didn't take her long to realize that it was more about listening and that he had a naturally good ear for music.

It was in the mornings at her home in Kaka Nagar that Naina Devi and her grandson really bonded and shared moments of leisure together. Her routine began with her *riyaz* or practice; first a series of rippling *taans* followed by a *tappa*, a supple exercise to open up the vocal chords. Now came the 'reward'—a spoonful of honey and ginger, a sweet and sticky healing unguent for the throat—and Baba loved to lick the spoon afterwards. Then came tea and discussions: she would describe the papers she was writing and (of course) Raag Rang and speak about her grandfather Keshub Chandra Sen. It is fascinating to see that in one sense her life had come full circle, she had returned to her Bengali roots. She studied his papers and his writings carefully. She spoke of how this leader of the Brahmo Samaj had been misunderstood; that as a great reformist he was ahead of his time; that the controversial Cooch Behar marriage was totally misinterpreted and the stories about it were totally untrue. Indeed, there was something almost defensive about her stance.

But never once did she disclose to Baba what had happened in the family after her husband's death. Some older people have almost a fetish for describing their personal woes; she had a talent for suppressing hers. It was something to block out almost as if it had never existed. Her concerns were more about music, and these were the topics discussed in her daily telephone calls with her friends and protégées. The calls would last for an hour, sometimes more; very often they were about a specific performance, its strengths and shortfalls. Baba noticed that her opinions had become more set and strongly expressed, especially about music, unlike her younger, more malleable days; yet the laughter remained, the humour was very much alive, the warm affection that was like a magnet to most people was still there. But nothing was allowed to impinge on her personal space.

Of course there was the preoccupation with Raag Rang, a feeling that was both obsessive and possessive. She feared for its future as she would for a child that she herself had nourished. As she grew older, she knew that one day she would have to give up its charge to a younger person— but would it be somebody who shared her vision? It was her most poignant question to Baba: 'Can you carry Raag Rang for me, I know you are studying but do you have an interest, this is my one thing, can you carry that?'

Scarcely out of boyhood, how could he answer, except to stammer, 'I don't know'. And her statement that was almost a plea: 'This is my one thing: can you carry that?'

That question: how she must have gone on a mission to seek the person who could carry that 'one thing'. And how difficult to even begin to search. That 'one thing' was a legacy she hoped would be her musical bequest to the world. Her practical self told her how ephemeral was that hope in the face of a rapidly changing world.

Age was not on her side and now increasingly neither was her health. Her first stroke came in the late 1980s, an indication of the toll that time and events had taken on her physical being. She must have been aware of what was happening to her and she chose to combat her condition by refusing to accept it. By now she had begun to lose her voice; this, too, was pushed aside, though she must have heard it in her morning *riyaz*. Her health was having an effect on her personality as she became more and more headstrong in her actions. A second stroke followed and then a public embarrassment; almost straight from the hospital she went to perform in a Ghalib-based programme. Her voice had deteriorated further and the audience could hear it; somehow, she could not; and unfortunately the concert was a disaster. In fact members of the family were scolded for allowing this to happen; how could you let her sing like this, they were asked, you people are so cruel. But nobody realized that it was she who was insistent that she would sing and refused to listen to the advice of her son and daughter. Sadly, this was to be her last public performance.

It had come to a stage where she was unwilling to accept what was happening to her. Her only response was a kind of bewildered anger. The family turned to Baba for help, thinking that he was the only person to whom, perhaps, she might listen. In one of their morning tea sessions he broached the subject gently. Maybe, he suggested, you should think of not singing any more in public, your voice is not what it used to be. He could tell by her expressionless face that she was deeply hurt. The result was that she became even more adamant in her actions and opinions. Through all those years of pain and struggle it was her music that had carried her, she had blocked out her problems and the compromises that she was forced to make in her life by pushing herself deeper and deeper into music; and now, even that was being taken away from her.

Raag Rang was always at the top of her mind; once, when she was in hospital she insisted on attending one of its concerts and had to be taken to the auditorium attached to a drip with a nurse in tow. This attracted more criticism for the family; of course, the outside world was not aware of that iron determination and will power that brooked no opposition.

She cut down on her activities and started going out less. The morning round of telephone calls dropped in frequency and number: Baba could hear the loneliness in her voice as she chided someone, 'You don't call me anymore!' Fewer people came to visit, although her students were always there. She was not getting the attention that she got earlier during the heady days of Raag Rang at its peak; she was no longer at the centre of things and a certain emptiness set in; by now she was becoming more aware of her own physical frailty. The fate of Raag Rang continued to be a major concern and occupied her thoughts.

The third stroke was the fatal one. She and Baba had just finished dinner; he noticed that she was trying to say something. She pointed to the jar of glucose and he gave her a spoon of it. A little later he saw that her mouth was drooping and went to the phone to call his cousins: but she clung to his hand as if begging him not to call, she did not want to go into hospital again.

A few days later she passed away, still in the Intensive Care Unit of the hospital.

But the dancer, Uma Sharma, a protégée who was a dear friend, remembers well the morning of that same day. She received a telephone call from Naina Devi to tell her that she had found an old cassette of her recordings and that she should come over so that they could listen to it together. For two hours

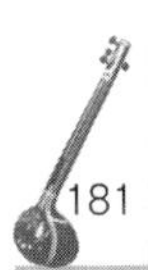

Naina Devi's great grandsons, Dhairyajit and Shauryajit, pay their homage at her samadhi in Rajanagar

they listened to the music playing back from that small tape player, Naina Devi singing all the forms she was so famous for, *thumri* and ghazal, *dadra* and *holi* and *chaiti*...they soaked in that glorious voice, the skills, the emotions, the range of repertoire. The session ended because Uma had to go elsewhere but she promised she would return later in the day. In the afternoon she got a call saying that Naina Devi had a stroke and was in hospital. She never saw her again, and her sense of bereavement was intense.

Naina Devi, captured at a sublime moment

But for Uma those magic two hours represented a precious memory: as if at her time of departure, she wanted to share her music with her friend as a way of saying farewell. For Naina Devi herself there could have been no better way to go, listening once more to her own voice in its pure and flawless prime, floating out of life on sublime clouds of music.

***

EPILOGUE

A Tribute to My Grandmother

Chandrajit Singh

How do you pay tribute to someone who has touched your life in myriad ways; whose presence continues to exert its influence, even with the passage of time? How do you remember someone who has never been forgotten, whose memory remains as fresh even after 24 years? Although my grandmother was an integral part of my childhood, the special bond that we shared developed at the time when I came to stay with her at D-II/59 Kaka Nagar in 1988 and continued till her demise in 1993. I had the privilege to share her existence and her space and be her trusted companion in the last years of her life. A privilege that I never really understood or appreciated at the time, but which I have grown to value over the years.

Naina Devi was steeped in music and music was her world. To call it her passion is an understatement. Music was the one constant in her life. It was her rock and the only thing which kept her going. My own interest in classical music drew me close to her, and her to me, and was the beginning of our deep association. Our conversations, invariably over morning tea or at dinner, covered a gamut of issues, including her musical experiences past and present, and her associations with the legends of yore, which spoke of her profound commitment to the cause of music. Out of this undying love was born Raag Rang, through which she showcased music the way she understood it and the way she believed to be important. It was an endeavour for which she expended all the energy and resources at her disposal. It was this zeal which defined her musical journey not only as a musician or a musicologist, but more importantly as a devoted patron. I saw my grandmother in the way she wanted to be seen. In her eyes she was neither Nilina Sen nor Rani Nina Ripjit Singh but only Naina Devi, an identity which she had created, which she had nurtured and which she had to endure. Neither the trials and tribulations of the past nor her personal strife could rob her of this identity which she had adorned. This was her refuge and music was her sanctuary. She was not defined by the aristocracy of her birth nor her marriage. Instead she had defined her own existence. She was only Naina Devi with her soul rooted in music.

What I admired the most about her was her dogged determination to keep on going. She was a fighter and remained so till the bitter end. She was such a soft and gentle person but at the same time incredibly strong. No one else but her could have survived the highs and lows, the blows which life had dealt her and still have emerged a winner. Her pride in whatever she did, her pride in her own existence, her dignity and the determination to live with her head held high defined her very character. Even when her voice began to fail her, she refused to let go. She struggled till her last breath, as she had done throughout her life.

She found her strength in spirituality. She was not a religious person and not one for rites and rituals. Nor was she drawn to any particular religion, but instead was deeply rooted in the philosophy of Sufism. From her I learnt to believe in the goodness of people. In her I saw an amazingly positive person who sincerely believed in harmony and peaceful coexistence. Her kindness and compassion knew no bounds. Having lived with her, I was witness to her empathy and her generosity to anyone who came for help, especially from the musical fraternity, regardless of rank or file. Whatever little she had was willingly shared with one and all. My greatest source of admiration for her came from the fact that in spite of the severe hardships that she had endured in her personal life there was no rancour or bitterness towards any one. In all our morning tête-à-têtes, rarely did she delve into the past or dwell on her struggles or her misfortunes. She never harboured an iota of ill will towards another living soul. That was her greatness. That was her goodness. That was who she was.

My grandmother was essentially a very lovable person. A joy to be with. She had such a wonderful sense of humour and the admirable quality to laugh at herself. The ability to put anyone at ease was an intrinsic part of her nature. After narrating an amusing anecdote, she would break into peals of laughter, which would resound within the walls of her Kaka Nagar home. The many amusing incidents and stories that we shared over fried fish and banana fritters are too many and too personal to relate. But perhaps the greatest tribute I can pay to her is to say that even as I think of her today after all these years, I do so with a smile on my face!

***

Women in Traditional Media

Naina Devi

Note: This paper is reproduced in its original version with its authentic style and formatting.

First presented at the consultation 'Empowering Women through Media', Bangalore, 1991.

Women, from time immemorial, have contributed to the human race's quest for knowledge, bringing to it their unique insights and natural empathy. In our country, their contribution has been quite exceptional, though acknowledged but in passing, like an afterthought. This is most unfortunate, for their value as singers has been seriously underestimated. They have been grudgingly acknowledged as very fine interpreters of lyrics, but seldom, if ever, as co-creators of a composition or 'Bandish'.

Our music, more than in any other country, when written is mere 'paper music', without blood, bones and muscles. It is in the 'Aadayegi' or the correct rendering that it miraculously springs to life, containing within it spontaneous improvisation beyond its immediate import. This is particularly true of what is termed as Light Classical Music — namely Thumri, Dadra, Tappa Kajri, Chaiti and Ghazal— where the words of a composition are inextricably linked with 'Sur', 'Lay' and 'Taal' and are enhanced, refined and made lovelier still.

Vocal music of this kind is redolent with emotions fragrances and… ideas. In other words it is an art of nuances where mere virtuosity can throw you completely off the scent. The lyrics being short, but with different connotations became an ideal vehicle for women to express their innermost thoughts and feelings.

Thumri and Dadra gained their pre-eminence in the court of Nawab Wajid Ali Shah, the last ruler of Avadh, over the last century or a little more. They gained their rightful place as genuine art forms within the mainstream of our classical music, much to the annoyance of the Pandits and Ustads who had scant regard for them as they felt that these smacked of Shringar Ras and hence frivolity! In their heart of hearts they felt deeply insulted, being practitioners of more edifying forms like Dhrupad, Dhamar, Khayal and Tarana. This, however, did not prevent them from singing this 'lighter' form of music with great relish, on the sly—in private. It was only later, around the First World War that Ustads sang them openly in their private and public concerts. Among the first performers were the great pioneer Bhaiya Ganpat Rao, the son of the ruler of Gwalior and Chandrabhaga Raj, a superb musician; his gifted pupil Moizuddin Khan of Banaras; Ustad Abdul Karim Khan of Kirana; and Sangeet Acharya Girija Shankar Chakravarthy of Calcutta. Subsequently, great musicians like Ustad Faiyaz Khan, Baba Nasir Khan, Ustad Bade Ghulam Ali Khan and his brother Ustad Barkat Ali Khan (more than any other male singer) excelled at Thumri singing.

But this form belonged rightfully to women. It will not be out of place to mention that according to the Natya Shastra, Dhruva Geet or expressive music has four 'vrittis' or characteristics. 'Kaishiki Vritti' which is 'komal' (delicate) and emotional suits the female voice. Therefore it can be said that Thumri is more suited to the female voice, perhaps this is the reason why this form of music was practiced by courtesans, tawaifs and baijis from Banaras, Lucknow and Gaya. It enabled them to musically emote the overwhelming injustice of their third class status as artistes and human beings, and also act as spokeswomen for their more economically privileged sisters imprisoned in the zenana, whose menfolk came to the kothas for an evening of diversion and entertainment.

Rarely did any man realise that there was more…much more to the content of the song than its immediate meaning.

The teachers were invariably male, usually musicians of some eminence, and in certain cases of considerable repute. They usually gave them systematic grounding in Hindustani classical music to express Rasa and Bhava, through judicious blending of Ragas.

Thumri is essentially 'shringar rasa pradhan abhinayatmak' sangeet, or that expressive and emotive music which is steeped in 'shringar rasa'. The Natya Shastra says: 'shyamo bhavathi shringara'. The colour of shringara is blue, symbolic of the vast expanse of infinity, like the ocean and the sky. The governing diety of shringara is Vishnu, who also has a blue complexion. Like the vastness of its symbolic blue colour, it covers the entire gamut of expression of human experience, from the sensuous to the sublime. The central 'Prem' includes milan, viraha, vatsalya, komalta and bhakti. There is no rasa known separately as Bhakti rasa. The theme of the lyrics also revolves around the episodes of Radha and Krishna or a lover and his beloved.

It must always be remembered, but for a moment of ecstasy with her beloved, Radha was an eternal Virahini, like most women of this world. It is this sense of loss that is so poignantly expressed in thumri. The thumri in Raag Pilu—'Tum Radhe Bana Shyam, hum Nandlala', when sung by a man is portrayed differently from that sung by a woman. There are 78 r.p.m. recordings of two versions available. The one sung with great verve by Ustad Barkat Ali Khan portrays the Ardha-Narishwar concept, saying that a man's personality also contains a feminine aspect and vice-versa. The second version by Indubala, a marvellous woman artiste of yesteryear, is quite simply a cry from the heart. The world then belonged to men, and unfortunately still does, to a large extent; it was alright for a man to be amorous for it was a proof of virility, but in a woman—a sure sign of promiscuity!

Then, as now, a woman was not expected to reveal her feelings. It did not matter that she carried a child in her womb for nine months, gave birth and reared it from infancy to adulthood and beyond. That she was the most stabilizing factor at home did not seem to matter. She was the plaything in the hands of the male, for he controlled the purse, the 'anndata'. It was especially these aspects that came through subtly and movingly in Thumri and Dadra. One arrived at reality through myth, usually the Radha-Krishna legend. The union with God and the sensuality of a physical union between a woman and a man – both these ideas are rendered as single identity with great depth of feeling and infinite delicacy by the gravely-ill Rasoolan Bai in her old age, her voice covering just one octave, fully aware of the responsibility of the task at hand.

May I at this juncture digress into autobiography and anecdotes? I am doing so with a purpose. Rasoolan Bai was one of my teachers and I learnt a lot from her. She came from an illustrious tradition of tawaifs and belonged to Banaras. A tradition that before her produced outstanding artistes like Gauhar Jaan, Janki Bai, Wazir Jaan, Malka Jaan, Vidhyadhari Bai, Rajeshwari Bai, amongst others. She was old, ill and practically destitute, bypassed by time, when she came and stayed with me. The cascading, sinuous voice of her youth had long since deserted her but the wisdom of her life-experience and her innate musicality and knowledge remained with her till the end. She showed how wonderfully expressive

musical things could be achieved with so little. A shining example is her 'chaiti', 'Yehi Thaiyan Motiya Hirae Gaieeli Rama, Kahewas Mein Dhundu...' A song portraying a newly married young girl, shyly but anxiously searching for a missing pearl of her nose-ring, the 'nath'. She looks for it all over the house, particularly her 'sej' (bed) after the previous night's love play. Her singing was so poignantly expressive, that we forgot her decrepit, old wrinkled face. She was transformed into a shy, blushing bride.

Talking about 'chaiti', I would like to explain what it is. It is seasonal folk music in origin, that has been stylized and is now included in the Dadra style of singing. Chaiti is sung after Phag and Holi, when spring has had its day and summer is fast approaching. The month of 'chait' lends an atmosphere of contentment and leisure and a feeling of langour in the air. The lyrics have a peculiar sensuous appeal, sung by women in a recollective mood of tranquility and fulfillment. They portray a 'Ratitripta Nayika'.

Rasoolan Bai's singing here, despite the tiredness of the voice, leaves mere virtuosity miles behind, it is as profound in its insights as it is fundamental in its musical quest. She now sang only for herself and her God, with whom she had a long-standing quarrel. In moments of exasperation she would ask if God was there and if so why was he so unkind to her. Was she angry because of the dichotomy that existed between the harsh, pitiless reality of life in an ever-changing world, and an exquisite private dream? A dream she voiced with such voluptuous purity in a thumri. I also had the privilege of knowing Badi Moti Bai of Banaras towards the end of her life. This stalwart of thumri, the only pupil of the legendary Moizuddin Khan, had by then become completely down and out. She was paralysed for fourteen years without any means of livelihood. She had come to know that the Union Ministry of Culture was giving pensions to eminent artistes and came to Delhi. She came and stayed with me. Her extraordinary will and urge for music made her able to sing again and proved she could so with excellence. The emotional integrity of Rasoolan Bai and Badi Moti Bai's music was truly astonishing. Both these great artistes excelled in 'bol-banana' or musically conveying the meaning of a word in different ways with different connotations, the main feature of the thumri style of singing.

The reason for mentioning these two female artistes is three-fold: personal, musical and sociological. They come from the tawaif tradition where a woman despite her brilliant accomplishments was never really secure. Unless she was very lucky, the caprices of a patron, the fickleness and dishonesty of a lover, not to forget silently creeping old age, would get her in the end. It would not then matter how delicately her imagination worked at Bol-banana or how proficiently her voice executed the essential quality of her vocal timbre exemplified by technique.

Vocalist Gangubai Hangal had once said 'If you are a man, you become a Pandit or Ustad but if you are a woman no matter how good you are, you are only a Bai!'

I, for one, turned to light classical music, because it offered me the scope to express myself more fully and also because I may have subconsciously felt a deep empathy for the women who enriched the tradition. On mature reflection in later years, I found this to be true.

I come from a liberal enlightened family. My grandfather, Keshub Chandra Sen, was a great social reformer and one of the pillars of the Brahmo Samaj in Bengal. My father was a barrister and played the violin, mother played the piano and the harmonium. My elder brother, Sunith Chandra Sen organised soirees of Hindustani classical music at home; and it was there that I first heard maestros such Inayat Khan, Hafiz Ali Khan, Zamiruddin Khan, Sangeet Acharya Girija Shankar Chakravarthy and many others. It was Girija Babu who, astonished at my perfectly reproducing a song that I had heard him sing, decided to teach me. My elder sister Sadhana, whom I called 'mejdi', and I became Girija Babu's disciples. Mejdi was a pioneer and later became famous as a modern ballet dancer and an actress in the films. Her husband Modhu Bose (my brother-in-law) was equally famous as a film director.

I was married off into the royal family of Kapurthala while still in my teens. It was no longer possible for me to study music. I sang to myself when alone in my room. There was no question of a Rani singing, even for her own pleasure! However there was music on festive occasions and mujras too. I listened to the music of the Bais in the mujras very attentively from the zenana.

My husband appreciated light classical styles of music and at the behest of Sunilda (Sunil Kumar Bose) of AIR Lucknow, I resumed my music practice. In fact in 1949, a year before his sad premature death, my husband urged me to cut four discs for the Columbia recording company that had a studio in Lucknow.

After my husband's death I returned increasingly to music for solace. In Thumri I found a vehicle for conveying my feelings. I was widely criticised, not only by the members of my family, but also by the so-called respectable society.

After all it was the music of Baijis, said so many. I wondered, if I had taken up Dhrupad or Khayal would I have been so rebuked?

I had the privilege of learning from a great musician like Ustad Mushtaq Hussain Khan of Rampur and also receiving guidance from other greats like Ustad Bade Ghulam Ali Khan, Ustad Hafiz Ali Khan and Anjani Bai Malpekar amongst others. My music has taught me to seek an accord between the finite and infinite and has made life, despite all its difficulties varied, rich and enjoyable.

The value of Bhava in Thumri and its natural link with Kathak dance opened new doors of perception for me, thanks to my association with that remarkable dancer Shambhu Maharaj, whose knowledge of both Kathak and Thumri was quite exceptional.

My travels as an artiste and as a consultant producer of Doordarshan have taught me a lot and opened new channels.

A particularly galling memory of official high-handedness comes back to me. An extremely puritanical politician declared a few years after Independence that all the Tawaifs and Bais be banned from singing on the radio and their records be destroyed immediately! He decreed that it was bad for the morale of the country to let disreputable women sing over AIR. The only way out was to produce marriage certificates stating that they were happily married housewives who sang for their pleasure alone! It did not occur to the worthy gentleman that the Radio was increasingly becoming a source of much needed income for these artistes and that traditional feudal patronage was falling off dramatically for historical reasons.

Overnight many Bais and Jaans became Devis and Begums much to the grim satisfaction of the government officials.

Why I took up the name of Naina Devi is of course another story. I could not sing under my own name because I did not want to offend my family members: so I sang incognito under the pseudonym Naina Devi. This makes me go back to my childhood. I vividly recall my childhood memories of Banaras. Early every morning my grandmother used to go to the Ahilyabai Ganga Ghat to bathe in the Ganga. I always accompanied her but while Didima bathed, I sat by a beggar woman who lived in one of the alcoves of the Ghat and sang:

'Hey Govind, hey Gopal, suniye Prabhu mori
Hey Govind rakho sharan ab to jeevan hare'

Help me Lord, I have lost the will to live. Her voice and her beautiful style of singing very similar to the Thumri haunted me. She had big black expressive eyes which were as haunting as her voice. I learnt later that the beggar woman was none other than a famous tawaif of Banaras who gave up the world and lived in the Ganga Ghat alcove. This left an indelible impact on my mind.

The tragedy of my husband's sudden death had completely broken me. I was only 29 years of age then. The latent impact of the beggar woman's voice on me, now came to the forefront and inspired me to take to this particular style of music and gave me the courage to sing publicly. I decided to take the name Naina Devi after her beautiful sad eyes.

I was often mistaken for a tawaif. Probably for my style of singing and my name. I even received an invitation for participating in a Tawaif Welfare Conference! It tickled me a lot but did not bother me. On the contrary I took it as a compliment that my music was as professional as a professional traditional singer.

To come to a full circle, it would not be wrong to say that the much maligned forms of light classical music lent beauty and substance to our musical tradition and added to the joy of living. Thumri, when sung by an experienced and gifted performer, reveals itself in its true colours—as essence of Dhrupad, Dhamar, Khayal and other pure classical styles. Its genuinely emotive character is best brought out by women singers who can effortlessly capture the fleeting beauty of the momentary and wed it to a universal human experience.

Singers or Musicians
Singers or Musicians

Integration, a Heritage of the Performing Arts

Naina Devi

Note: This paper is reproduced in its original version with its authentic style and formatting.

First presented in New Delhi on 15 April 1987.

'Like a bee collecting honey from flowers,
the intelligent shall glean truths from all scriptures great or small.'

—*Bhagvatam*

These lines from the Bhagavata epitomise the Indian approach to life in general and are equally true of the performing arts of India. Our culture has always had the capacity to absorb and assimilate different qualities and ideas. Our performing arts also reflect this. Like our religious tradition which allows each individual to choose his own path of worship within the prescribed discipline, our performing arts too give ample scope to each artiste to interpret and give expression to a basic idea in his own individual manner within the boundaries of the discipline of a classical form of music or dance. Freedom in discipline is a special Indian quality which is very difficult to achieve.

Music is not merely a means of entertainment, it is perhaps the most effective instrument for the sublime communion with the ultimate. It has been closely linked with worship and is an important part of the social and religious ceremonies of our country. 'Naad' is considered the Godhead made manifest as sound and great importance is attached to it in our philosophy and music. Ancient rituals are performed with Vedic chants of abstract sound and rhythmic metre without the use of words. Pleasing sound and vibrant rhythm appeal to all and know no barrier.

Our music of the northern part of the country, from Kashmir to Manipur and Assam has been greatly influenced by Vaishnavism and Sufism, both very similar in their concept and approach. We find that many styles have evolved and further developed from the Vaishnavite concept of the 'the lover and the beloved', symbolic of the yearning of the human soul to unite with the Universal soul, laying emphasis on 'Madhur Bhakti'. The same concept is found in many compositions of Sufi Saints.

Raag Rang and the Sangeet Natak Akademi had organised a festival called 'Bansuri' which focused on this idea. The festival was held in 1980 and had invited well-known litterateurs, Sufis, musicologists and performing artistes to a four-day seminar for detailed discussions and demonstrations. The styles evolved varied from folk to semi-classical and classical music, such as Sufiana Kalam, Baul, Kirtan, Haveli Sangeet, Kafi Qawwali, Thumri, Hori Dhammar, Khayal and Dhrupad.

Among instruments we find special importance being given by both streams of philosophy to the flute which is considered a symbol for the call of the soul. The special significance of the reed flute 'Bansuri' in Vaishnavite and Sufistic thought is expressed by poets such as Jaidev, Maulana Jalaluddin Rumi, Bihari, Chandidas to name a few.

A few couplets of Rumi:

Oh listen to the plaintive music of the flute
Wailing the pangs of separation
Embedded in the heart are the notes
That exude the anguished melody.
The plaintive melody is attuned to all
Those who rejoice, and those who weep
The lover who shreds his garments in frenzy
Cleanses himself of his greed and other impurities
Blessed is the madness of love
It has cured me of all my maladies.

—Translation by Naina Devi

The Flute Enchanting—Chandidas

How can I a lass so simple cope with the pranks of 'Kala'
The magic of his flute, O friend,
So overpowers me.

The chants of prayers and rituals
Seem but futile...
It resounds so strongly in my ears
I respond to nothing but
That haunting, enchanting music.
—*Translation by Naina Devi*

The other instruments are the sarod, sitar and the santoor. All these instruments have developed from instruments that were traditionally used for accompanying Sufiana Kalam. The word sarod means music in Persian, and the name rabab, the instrument from which the sarod has evolved, is devised from 'Rab' meaning God and 'Aab' meaning water conveying the idea that God's name flows like water.

A community of musicians known as Rababists sang Shabad Kirtan at Gurdwaras till as late as the Partition of India. They were all Muslims. The sitar is the developed form of the 'sehtar' still used by the Sufiana Kalam singers of Kashmir, and so is the Santoor. Santoor is a folk instrument which has very recently been adopted for classical music.

Haveli Sangeet, the Vaishnavite music sung in the Vaishnav monasteries of Udaipur, Gujarat and Braj is the mother of Dhrupad, Dhammar and Thumri. Dhrupad and Dhammar have been highly developed and stylised whereas Thumri retains some of its folk flavour. Qawwali of the Sufi Khanqahs has given birth to the Khayal, which is now a highly developed classical style. Kirtan of Bengal is a typical Vaishnavite congregational music which started from the time of Shri Chaitanya Deva (1485-1533) and blossomed out into many varieties which have their own disciplines. Baul of Bengal expresses the Vaishnav and the Sufi concepts in their own respective disciplines.

When Khwaja Moinuddin Chishti came to India and settled in Ajmer (1142–1236) he came in contact with Indian music. Here, music occupied a pride of place and played a vital role in the social and religious life of the country. Impressed by this, he invented a fascinating blend of Arabic spiritual music known as 'Sama' and Indian music and called it Qawwali. The new syncretic music suited Indian culture and the temperament of the Indian people admirably and soon Qawwali became the most successful method of preaching the tenets of Sufism and the message of Islam. Qawwali has played a very important role in the lives of Sufi saints of the Chishtia order.

It was in the Khanqah of Khwaja Nizamuddin Aulia of Delhi that the great scholar-musician, Amir Khusro, composed beautiful 'bandishes' in Khari Boli, Brajbhasha and Persian. A Qawwali mehfil is claimed by Sufis to transcend their observations and experiences to the spiritual plane in a state of 'Kafiat' and 'Wajd', brought about by musical hypnosis. Khwaja Qutbuddin Bakhtiar Kaki remained in the blissful state of 'Wajd' for four days listening to the Qawwali.

Sarod cheest ke chandin
farsoon-e-ishq dar-oast
sarod mehram-e-ishq
asto-ishq mehram-e-oast

What is music? Why is it so enchanting?
Music is the secret of love, and love, the secret of God.

The Guru Granth Sahib has laid special emphasis on music. There is a chapter known as Ragamala which is solely devoted to music. Every shabad of this great book is set to a specific Raga. Guru Nanak Sahib's Arti in Raga Dhanasri is a striking example of a very broad vision for the glorification of the Universal Presence:

The sun and the moon oh Lord are Thy lamps
The firmament Thy salver
The orbs of the stars the pearls encased in it
The perfume of the sandal is Thine incense
The wind is Thy fan, all the forests are Thy flowers
Oh Lord of Lights what worship is This!
Thou Destroyer of Birth,
Unbeaten strains of ecstasy,
Are the trumpets of Thy worship.

The classical dance form of the North, Kathak, has imbibed the best of the two great cultures that influenced our country. Pirouettes peculiar to this dance form are symbolic of the cycle of life as well as of the Sufi concept of the whirling dance of the dervishes known as Maulawi. The meaning of this sufi dance is: Whichever way you may turn, you face God.

The pose typical of Kathak, the right hand pointing upwards and the left downwards, is also very similar to the hand gestures of Maulawi dance, meaning: Receive from Allah and give to the world.

Uday Shankar, the father of modern Indian ballet, developed an eclectic form out of a fusion of Kathakali, Manipuri, Bharatanatyam and Kathak. Sadhona Bose, also a great exponent of modern Indian dance, choreographed a dance number 'Divine Source' projecting the idea of integration as far back as 1944. The synopsis of the dance: A quarrel takes place among the dancers of the four major classical dance forms, Bharatanatyam, Kathakali, Manipuri and Kathak, arguing the merits of each by demonstrating their own proficiency. The quarrel rises to a high pitch and the dancers in desperation pray to Nataraj, Lord of the Dance, to mediate. Nataraj explains to them that there is one Divine Source of all dance forms, and each style is but a part of the whole divine message of the art of dance. The finale is reached by all the dancers putting aside their differences and rendering homage in unison to the Divine Source.

We are meeting here in 1987 to discuss an issue of vital importance to our nation as well as to our performing arts. It is important that at this juncture we should consider these issues because of the increasing focus by the younger generation on religions, sects, groups etc., all of which create an atmosphere of discord. The idea that these divisions are artificial, the notion of different voices expressing the same truth, has always been a part of our tradition and has always found expression in our performing arts. Bade Ghulam Ali Khan's 'Hari Om Tatsat' is still remembered with nostalgia by those who heard him and Kumar Gandharva continues to sing 'Qutabuddin Qutabalam'. We are therefore only carrying forward the work of our forefathers.

I end my paper with my grandfather's last speech in 1883:

> Let all sects retain their distinctive peculiarities, and yet let them unite in fraternal alliance. The unity I content for is the unity of music. There is concordance in the midst of apparent discordance. Each instrument has its own individuality, its specific character; each voice retains its peculiar tone, yet out of the union of many voices and diverse instruments comes forth sweet and delicious music.
>
> (Keshub Chandra Sen, 23 January 1883)

***

Endnotes

Note: Sources of quoted material are indicated by page number and an identifying phrase from the text. Complete information about the sources is provided in the Bibliography.

INTRODUCTION

P. 15: 'We know people…'	Tagore, 1921, pp. 147–48.

NILINA SEN: CALCUTTA 1917–1935

P. 21: 'banians'	Sarkar, 2013, p. 450.
P. 26: 'to entertain lavishly…'	Banerjee, 1998, p. 24.
P. 26: '…thanked her in very…'	Dutta, 2003, p. 30.
P. 28: 'Looking back on those…'	Devee, 1921, pp. 16–17.
P. 31: 'nurse of sciences…'	
'inventress of delightful and useful arts'	Asiatic Society, 1784.
P. 31: 'We are like savages…'	Raghavan, n.d., p. 2.
P. 32: '…a class of persons…'	Macaulay, 1835.
P. 35: 'wonderful mastery of…'	Poddar, 1977, p. 59.
P. 35: 'when he spoke…'	Kopf 1979, p. 205.
'a tall princely man…'	Kopf 1979, p. 255.
'a saintly youth'	Kopf 1979, p. 257.
'to me dearer…'	Kopf 1979, p. 257.
P. 36: 'the worship and adoration…'	Trust deed of Brahmo Sabha.
Pp. 37–38: 'He must have…grew well again.'	Devee, 1921, pp. 3–6.

P. 38: 'a being exhausting itself...'	Poddar, 1977, p. 47.
P. 39: 'the brightest jewel...'	Poddar, 1977, p 41.
P. 39: 'paying reverence to...'	Kopf, 1979, p. 136.
P. 39: 'If England seeks to...'	Poddar, 1977, p. 52.
P. 40: 'I came here...'	Poddar, 1977, p. 54.
P. 42: 'My antagonists have...'	Devee, 1921, p. 71.
P. 44: 'The attraction was...'	Kopf, 1979, p. 265.
'If God is father-like...'	Kopf, 1979, p. 277.
'Now that I have seen...'	Kopf, 1979, p. 280.
P. 45: 'To me the state...'	Kopf, 1979, p. 254.
P. 45: 'I loved that hour...'	Devee, 1921, p. 18.
P. 46: 'exacted and received...'	Devee, 1921, p. 17.
P. 46: 'I have another...'	Devee, 1921, pp. 24–25.
P. 48: 'We tried to persuade ...'	Devee, 1921, pp. 30–31.
P. 49: 'Many distinguished visitors...'	Devi, 1966, p. 21.
P. 51: 'Unless my sisters marry...'	Devee, 1921, p. 164.

RANI NINA RIPJIT SINGH: SIMLA, RAJANAGAR, DELHI, AWADH: 1935–1953

P. 69: 'flower gardens with...'	Bhasin, 1992, p. 131.
P. 70: 'Sirdar Charanjit Singh of...'	Harris, 2005, p. 85.
P. 74: 'Next to diamonds...'	Mathur, 2004, p. 47.
P. 75: 'a docile population...'	Kanwar, 1990, p. 36.
P. 76: 'While in 1814...'	Kanwar, 1990, p. 33.
P. 77: 'Here you are...'	Kanwar, 1990, p. 35.
P. 77: 'I believe we will...'	Buck, 1925, p. 36.
P. 79: 'The East is a university...'	Cavendish, 1999, p. 1.
P. 79: 'The delay is bad...'	Buck, 1925, p. 56.
'I agree with the...'	Buck, 1925, p. 56.
P. 80: 'I do not know for...'	Devee, 1921, p. 145.
P. 81: 'hang about'	Kanwar, 1990, p. 98.
P. 81: 'both have now spent...'	Kanwar, 1990, p. 102.

P. 81: 'On three sides...'	Buck, 1925, p. 175.
P. 86: 'When I realized...'	Kopf, 1979, p. 299.
P. 88: 'eminently suitable for the...'	Kanwar, 1990, p. 102.
P. 88: 'The panelling, false ceiling...'	Bhasin, 1992, p. 21.
P. 89: 'Not one benefit...'	Gleig, 1879, p. 182.
P. 110: 'a bit of bunting'	Codell, 2012.
P. 110: 'Now...we do by these...and on our behalf...'	Queen Victoria's Proclamation, p. 2.
P. 111: 'Curzonation Durbar'	Codell, 2012, p. 5.
'an extravagant waste'	Codell, 2012, p. 6.
'a glorified bazaar'	Codell, 2012, p. 6.
P. 112: '100,000 people'	Codell, 2012, p. 6.
P. 113: 'long...recognised to be...'	Wright, 2011.
P. 113: 'Delhi is still...'	Pothen 2012, p. 24.
P. 113: '...these ancient walls...'	Pothen, 2012, p. 25.
P. 114: 'British rule in...'	Pothen, 2012, p. 28.
P. 114: 'too wooden, too iron...'	Singh, 1973, p. 1.
'increasing association of Indians...'	Singh, 1973, p. 2.
P. 115: 'In as much as...'	Singh, 1973, p. 4.
'a safety valve for...'	Singh, 1973, p. 3.
P. 119: 'The sensuous life...'	Mukherjee, 2002, p. 33.
'a cherry which will...'	Mukherjee, 2002, p. 32.
P. 120: 'This life of Lucknow...'	Sharaar, 1994, Introduction, p. 13.
P. 124: '...the courtesans were...'	Graf (ed.) 1997, p. 139.
P. 124: '...it was said that...'	Sharaar, 1994, p. 192.
P. 127: '...solid as a rock...'	Bhasin, 1992, p. 345.

NAINA DEVI: DELHI: 1953–1993

P. 138: '...a brief memory from...'	Interview with Partho Basu, *Illustrated Weekly of India*, 1983.
P. 145: 'I helped financially.'	Khokhar, p. 52.
P. 150: '*Main koi rundee...*'	Mukherji, 2006, p. 136.

P. 156: 'How is this wedding going…'	Personal interview with a family member.
P. 165: 'to propagate the…'	Taken from Raag Rang anniversary brochure, 1962–1972.
P. 172: 'What are you doing?'	Personal interview with a family member.
P. 173: '…sung in an intensely lyrical…'	Taken from Raag Rang anniversary brochure, 1962–1972, reproduced from column by the music critic of *The Statesman*, 19 April 1963.

***

Select Bibliography

Banerjee, Sumanta. *The Parlour and the Streets: Elite and Popular Culture in 19th century Calcutta*. Calcutta: Seagull Books, 1998.

Bhasin, Raaja. *Simla: the Summer Capital of British India*. New Delhi: Viking India, 1992.

Buck, Sir Edward John. *Simla Past and Present*. Bombay: The Times Press, 1925.

Cavendish, Richard. 'Lord Curzon Takes Office as Viceroy of India.' *History Today* 49/1, 1999. http://www.historytoday.com/richard-cavendish/lord-curzon-takes-office-viceroy-india (accessed 27 July 2017).

Chaudhuri, Sukanta, ed. *Calcutta, a Living City, Vols 1 and 2*. Delhi: Oxford University Press India, 1990.

Codell, Julie, 'On the Delhi Coronation Durbars, 1877, 1903, 1911.' http://www.branchcollective.org/?ps_articles=julie-codell-on-the-delhi-coronation-durbars-1877-1903-1911 (accessed 27 July 2017).

Devee, Sunity (Suniti Devi), Maharani of Cooch Behar. *The Autobiography of an Indian Princess*. London: John Murray, 1921.

Devi, Rani Saheba Joyoti. *Sucharu Devi, Maharani of Mourbhanj*. Translated from Bengali by Prabhat Bose. Calcutta: Sree Saraswati Press Ltd, 1966.

Dutta, Krishna. *Calcutta: A Cultural and Literary History*. Calcutta: Signal Books, 2003.

Gleig, G.R, and Sir R. H. Sale. *Sale's Brigade in Afghanistan, with an Account of the Seizure and Defence of Jellalabad*. London: John Murray, 1879. https://archive.org/stream/salesbrigadeinaf00glei/salesbrigadeinaf00glei_djvu.txt (accessed 27 July 2017).

Graf, Violette, ed. *Lucknow: Memories of a City*: Delhi: Oxford University Press India, 1997.

Harris, Russell. *The Lafayette Studio and Princely India*. New Delhi: Lustre Press/ Roli Books, 2005.

Jhala, Angma Dey. *Courtly Indian Women in Late Imperial India*. London: Pickering & Chatto, 2008.

———. *Royal Patronage, Power and Aesthetics in Princely India*. London: Pickering & Chatto, 2011.

Kanwar, Pamela. *Simla: Imperial City: Political Culture of the Raj*. Delhi: Oxford University Press, 1990.

Khan, Moinuz Zafar. *The Council of State as a Second Chamber (1921-1947)*. New Delhi: Asia Publishing House, 1974.

Khokhar, Ashish. *Shriram Bharatiya Kala Kendra, A History*. New Delhi: Lustre Press/Roli Books. nd.

Kopf, David. *The Brahmo Samaj and the Shaping of the Modern Indian Mind*. Princeton: Princeton University Press, 1979.

Llewellyn-Jones, Rosie. *The Last King in India*. London: Hurst Publications, 2014.

Macaulay, T.B. 'Minute by the Hon'ble T. B. Macaulay, dated the 2nd February 1835.' http://www.columbia.edu/itc/mealac/pritchett/00generallinks/macaulay/txt_minute_education_1835.html (accessed 27 July 2017).

Mathur, AshaRani. *Indian Shawls: Mantles of Splendour*. New Delhi: Rupa & Co., 2004.

Mukherjee, Rudrangshu. *Awadh in Revolt: A Study in Resistance*. Delhi: Permanent Black India, 2002.

Mukherji, Kumar Prasada. *The Lost World of Hindustani Music*. Delhi: Penguin India, 2006.

Poddar, Arabinda. *Renaissance in Bengal*. Simla: Indian Institute of Advanced Study, 1977.

Pothen, Nayantara. *Glittering Decades, New Delhi in Love and War*. New Delhi: Penguin Viking, 2012.

Raghavan, Anirudh. 'British Orientalism in India: Nature and Impact on Indian Society (A Historiographical Survey)' nd. https://www.academia.edu/2565126/British_Orientalism_in_India_Nature_and_Impact_on_Indian_Society_A_Historiographical_Survey (accessed 27 July 2017).

Rao, Maya. *Maya Rao: A Lifetime in Choreography*. Bengaluru: Department of Kannada and Culture, Government of Karnataka, in collaboration with the Natya Institute of Kathak and Choreography, 2014.

Rao, Vidya. *Heart to Heart: Remembering Nainaji.* New Delhi: HarperCollins, 2011.

Sarkar, Suvobrata. 'Bengali Entrepreneurs and Western Technology in the Nineteenth Century: A Social Perspective.' *Indian Journal of History of Science,* 48.3 (2013): 447–75. http://www.insa.nic.in/writereaddata/UpLoadedFiles/IJHS/Vol48_3_4_SSarkar.pdf (accessed 27 July 2017).

Shah, Vidya. *Jalsa: Indian Women and their Journeys from the Salon to the Studio.* New Delhi: Tulika Books, 2016.

Sharar, Abdul Halim. *Lucknow: The Last Phase of an Oriental Culture.* Delhi: Oxford University Press India, 1994.

Singh, Bhawani. *Councils of State in India, a structural and functional profile.* Meerut: Meenakshi Prakashan, 1973.

Tagore, Rabindranath. *Glimpses of Bengal: Selected from the Letters of Sir Rabindranath Tagore 1885 to 1895.* London: Macmillan & Co., 1921.

Wright, Tom. 'Why Delhi? The Move from Calcutta. *The Wall Street Journal,* 11 November 2011. https://blogs.wsj.com/indiarealtime/2011/11/11/why-delhi-the-move-from-calcutta/ (accessed 27 July 2017).

Other web resources:

Asiatic Society: https://asiaticsocietycal.com/history/index.htm (accessed 27 July 2017).

Queen Victoria's Proclamation: http://www.csas.ed.ac.uk/mutiny/confpapers/Queen%27sProclamation.pdf (accessed 27 July 2017).

Trust deed of Brahmo Sabha: http://www.thebrahmosamaj.net/samajes/trustdeed.html (accessed 27 July 2017).

Text and Image Credits

Excerpt on p. 142 from *Maya Rao: A Lifetime in Choreography* by Maya Rao (Department of Kannada and Culture, Government of Karnataka, in collaboration with the Natya Institute of Kathak and Choreography, 2014) reproduced with kind permission from Smt Madhu Natraj, Director, Natya Institute of Kathak and Choreography.

Excerpt on p. 155 from *Heart to Heart: Remembering Nainaji* by Vidya Rao (Harper Collins Publishers India, New Delhi, 2011) reproduced with kind permission from the author.

All photographs © Rena Ripjit Singh, except for the ones listed below:

P. 143: Photograph © Shobha Deepak Singh; reproduced with her permission.

P. 18: Rabindranath Tagore, *My Reminiscences*, (p. 121), watercolour; public domain, https://commons.wikimedia.org/wiki/File:My_Reminiscences_p121.jpg.

P. 21: View of Fort William done after the painting in the Court Room of the Company's house in Leaden Hall Street, mezzotint, 1735; public domain, https://commons.wikimedia.org/wiki/File:Fort_William,_Calcutta,_1735.jpg.

P. 22: 'A Plan of the Battle of Plassey, fought 23 June 1757 by Col. Robt. Clive, against the Nabob of Bengal', circa 1760; public domain, https://commons.wikimedia.org/wiki/File:Plassey1757max.jpg.

P. 23: Benjamin West, 'Shah Alam II, Mughal Emperor, Conveying the Grant of the Diwani to Lord Clive, August 1765', Oil painting, 1818; public domain, https://commons.wikimedia.org/wiki/File:Shah_Alam_II,_Mughal_Emperor,_Conveying_the_Grant_of_the_Diwani_to_Lord_Clive,_August_1765.jpg.

P. 23: 'Clive examining the enemy lines from the roof of the Navab's hunting lodge'; public domain, http://www.columbia.edu/itc/mealac/pritchett/00routesdata/1700_2799 / companyrule/clive/clive.html.

P. 24: Calcutta, view of sailing ships and other boats docked along the River Hooghly, (unknown date); public domain, https://commons.wikimedia.org/wiki/File:Calcutta_view_-_sailing_ships_and_other_boats_docked_along_River_Hooghly_(unknown_date).jpg.

P. 25: Idol of the Goddess Durga during Durga Puja celebrations at Sovabazar, Calcutta; Jyotirmoydeb; public domain, https://commons.wikimedia.org/wiki/File:Sovabazar_Durga.jpg.

P. 30: James Posselwhite, Portrait of Sir William Jones (1746-1794), steel engraving, 19th century; public domain, https://commons.wikimedia.org/wiki/File:Sir_William_Jones.jpg.

P. 33: Raja Ram Mohan Roy, statue at College Green, Bristol; NotFromUtrecht; [CC BY-SA 3.0], https://commons.wikimedia.org/wiki/File:Ram_Mohan_Roy.jpg.

P. 33: Ishwar Chandra Vidyasagar, Portrait taken before 1891; public domain, https://commons.wikimedia.org/wiki/File:Ishwar_Chandra_Vidyasagar.jpg.

P. 33: Bankim Chandra Chatterjee from *The Literature of Bengal*, 1895, Romesh Chunder Dutt; public domain, https://commons.wikimedia.org/wiki/File:Bankim_Chandra_Chatterjee_from_The_Literature_of_Bengal.jpg.

P. 33: Rabindranath Tagore, before 1941, public domain, https://commons.wikimedia.org/wiki/File:Rabindranath_Tagore_unknown_location.jpg.

P. 33: Sarat Chandra Chatterjee, public domain, https://commons.wikimedia.org/wiki/File:Sharat_Chandra_Chatterji.jpg.

P. 35: Debendranath Tagore by Abanindranath Tagore; public domain, https://commons.wikimedia.org/wiki/File:Debendranath_Tagore.jpg.

P. 35: Bust of Dwarkanath Tagore at the National Library, Kolkata; Arjun Sarup; public domain, https://commons.wikimedia.org/wiki/File:Dwarkanath_Tagore_National_Library.png.

P. 43: Ramakrishna in a trance (state of samadhi) supported by his nephew Hriday and surrounded by Brahmo devotees. At the house of Keshub Chandra Sen, Calcutta 21 September 1879; public domain; https://commons.wikimedia.org/wiki/File:Ramakrishna_trance_1879.jpg.

P. 44: Swami Vivekananda, September, 1893, Chicago; Dziewa; public domain, https://commons.wikimedia.org/wiki/File:Swami_Vivekananda-1893-09-signed.jpg.

P. 66: Rabindranath Tagore, My *Reminiscences*, (p. 35), watercolour; public domain, https://commons.wikimedia.org/wiki/File:My_Reminiscences_p35.jpg.

P. 69: Kalka-Simla Railway, a passenger train on one of the smaller bridges; A.M.Hurrell; [CC BY-SA 3.0], https://commons.wikimedia.org/wiki/File%3AKSR_Train_on_a_small_bridge_05-02-12_52.jpeg.

P. 76: Maharaja Ranjit Singh, 1830, by Leopold Massard; World Sikh News; public domain, https://commons.wikimedia.org/wiki/File:MaharajaRanjitSIngh_-_L_Massard.gif.

P. 77: John Lawrence, 1st Baron Lawrence, c. 1895; Maull and Polybank; public domain, https://en.wikipedia.org/wiki/File:John_Lawrence_by_Maull_and_Polybank.jpg.

P. 78: The Gaiety Heritage Cultural Complex in Simla, on The Ridge; Biswarup Ganguly; [CC BY 3.0], https://commons.wikimedia.org/wiki/File:Gaiety_Theater_-_Ridge_-_Shimla_2014-05-07_1103.JPG

P. 80: The Viceregal lodge, Simla; Rishabh sharma007; [CC BY-SA 4.0], https://commons.wikimedia.org/wiki/File:Indian_Institute_of_Advanced_Study_Shimla.jpg.

P. 110. The Viceroy's House, Rashtrapati Bhavan in Delhi; AKS.9955; [CC BY-SA 4.0], https://commons.wikimedia.org/wiki/File:Rashtrapati_Bhavan_gate_close_up.jpg.

P. 112: Delhi Durbar, 1911; author unknown; public domain, https://commons.wikimedia.org/wiki/File:Delhi_Durbar,_1911.jpg.

P. 113: The Nizam of Hyderabad, Osman Ali Khan, Asif Jah VII, pays homage to King George V and Queen Mary at the Delhi Durbar, 1911; author unknown; public domain, https://commons.wikimedia.org/wiki/File:The_Nizam_of_Hyderabad_pays_homage_to_the_king_and_queen_at_the_Delhi_Durbar.jpg.

P. 119: Nawab Wajid Ali Shah, an engraving from 1872; author unknown; public domain, https://commons.wikimedia.org/wiki/File:Vajid_Ali_Shah.jpg.

P. 127: Pandit Vishnu Narayan Bhatkande; author unknown; public domain, https://commons.wikimedia.org/wiki/File:Bhatkhande.jpg.

P. 136: Rabindranath Tagore, My *Reminiscences*, (p. 99), watercolour; public domain, https://commons.wikimedia.org/wiki/File:My_Reminiscences_p99.jpg.

P. 161: Gauhar Jaan; author unknown; public domain, https://upload.wikimedia.org/wikipedia/commons/4/48/Gauhar_Jaan.jpg.

P. 162: Jaddan Bai; author unknown; public domain, https://commons.wikimedia.org/wiki/File:Jaddan_Bai_(1932).jpg.

P. 164: Begum Rafat Zamani of Rampur; author unknown; public domain, https://commons.wikimedia.org/wiki/File:Princess-rafat-zamani-begum.jpg

P. 184: Rabindranath Tagore, My *Reminiscences*, (p. 135), watercolour; public domain, https://commons.wikimedia.org/wiki/File:My_Reminiscences_p135.jpg.

P. 188: Dancing Girl by Tilly Kettle, oil on canvas; public domain; https://commons.wikimedia.org/wiki/File:Tilly_Kettle_-_Dancing_Girl_-_Google_Art_Project.jpg.

P. 196: Indian musicians and singers, Gouache drawing, attributed to a painter from Tanjore ca. 1840; Wellcome Trust; [CC BY 4.0], https://commons.wikimedia.org/wiki/File:Indian_musicians_and_singers._Gouache_drawing._Wellcome_V0045295.jpg.

***

Index

A

Abhinoy, 59
Abhisar, 60
Adi Brahmo Samaj, 34, 36
Ahmed, Maulvi Shah Niaz, *153*
Ajanta, 60
Ali Baba, 58, 59
Allahabad, 128, 133
Allahabadi, Janki Bai, 162
All India Muslim League, 128
All India Radio, 14, 126, 133
Ambala, 68
Amherst, Lord, 75
Andrews, Colonel William, 101
Anglo-Afghan War, 89
Anglo-Sikh wars, 75–76
Asiatic Society, 29, 31, 32
Awadh, 26, 65, 67, 77, 83, 87, 93, 117–127

B

Babu Culture, 26, 27
Babu, Girija, 52, 55–56, 127, 150, 177
Bagchi, Guru Taraknath, 55
Bai, Badi Moti, 169, 173
Bai, Jaddan, 161–162
Bai, Rasoolan, 166–169
baiji, 56, 122–124
banians, 21, 23
baramasa, 13
basant, 13
Battle of Buxar, 22, 117–118
Battle of Plassey, 22
Bengal Renaissance, 16, 27, 28, 31, 32
Bengal Social Science Association, 27
Bentinck, Lord, 75
Bharatiya Kala Kendra, 139–142
Bhookh, 60
Black Hole of Calcutta, 22
Bose, Sadhona, 15, 50–62
Brahmo Marriage Act, 40–41
Brahmo Samaj, 16, 28, 33–35
  splitting of, 85
Brahmo Samaj of India, 34, 39
British East India Company, 20 22, 23, 25, 74, 75, 89, 111, 117–119
Bushahr, 74

C

Cabinet Mission, 128–129
Calcutta
  British masters, 26
  fort, building, 21–22
  parties in, 26, 27
  trading, 20–21
Calcutta Medical College, 30
Calcutta Public Library, 27
Calcutta School Book Society, 27
Chadwick, 81–88
Chaitanya movement, 39
chaiti, 13, 123
Chakma, Raj, 52–53
Chakravarty, Girija Shankar, 16, 52, 55–56
Chapslee, 88–95
  memory of, 146
Charat Ram, Sumitra, 135, 139–140, 164
Chatterjee, Bankim Chandra, 33
Chatterjee, Sarat Chandra, 33
Chelmsford, Lady, 82
chilmans, 123–124
Christianity, 38–39
Clive, Robert, 23–25
Cooch Behar, 14, 16, 28, 30, 40–41, 47, 179
Curzon, Lord, 78–79, 80, 92, 111

D

Dadra, 122, 127, 182, 189–191
Dalia, 59
dar behest, 163
Datta, Narendranath, 44
Deb, Nabakrishna, 24–25
Delhi, Durbars, 104–117
Devi, Jaganmohini, 50
Devi, Naina, 138–139, 189–195
  about, 14–17
  arts, 197–201
  Bharatiya Kala Kendra, 139–142
  Kathak, 158–160
  last years of, 178–183
  personal life, 14–16
  Pusa Road, 142–150
  Raag Rang 1, 164–169
  Raag Rang 2, 172–178
  Rampur, 160–164
  to Simla, 16–17
Devi, Purnima, 85, 86
Devi, Siddheshwari, 144, 167–169
Devi, Sucharu (Maharani of Mayurbhanj), 16, 47–49
Devi, Suniti (Maharani of Cooch Behar), 14, 16, 28–29, 45–47, 49, 51, 80
  autobiography, 28, 37–38, 43, 45–47, 51, 80
dewani, 22
dewans, 23
dhamar, 55
dhrupad, 55
dobhashi, 24
Doordarshan, 14, 166, 168
Durbars, Delhi, 104–117
Durga Puja, 25–26

E

East India Company, *see* British East India Company
Ellenborough, Lord, 89
English-Bengali dictionary, 30
Executive Council, 69, 128

F

Fakhar-e-Jahan, Hazrat Maulana, 153
farmans, 20
foreign trading company, 20–21
Fort William, 21–23

G

Gaiety Theatre, Simla, 78
Gariffa, 29
Garika, 53
Ghosh, Pandit Pannalal, 140
ghungroos, 62
Gobindapur, 21
Goswami, Radhika Prasad, 55
Gurkhas, 74–75
gurudakshina, 62

H

habshi halwa, 163
Hindu College, 27, 30, 32
Holi, 26, 121, 122
Hooghly River, 21, 24, 29, 111
Hoshiarpur, 83

I

Imperial Civil Service (ICS), 62, 85
Indian Museum, 30
Indian Red Cross Society, 49

J

Jaan, Gauhar, 161
Jalsaghar, 27
Jhankar Music Circle, 140–141
jhoola, 13
Jones, William, 30, 31
Joshi, Nirmala, 140–141
jugalbandi, 177 –178
Jullunder (Jalandhar), 71, 83

K

Kaiser-i-Hind medal, 86
kajri, 13, 123
Kalikata, 21
Kalka, 68–69
Kalutola, 23, 28
Kaptai Dam, 53
Kapurthala, 14, 16, 62, 70, 80, 82–83, 148
Karna, Rani, 145
Kathak, 55, 61, 140, 144–145, 158–160, 174
Ker, Sir Arthur Milford, 92

Khan, Amjad Ali, 143
Khan, Rahmat Ali, 143
Khan, Ustad Allauddin, 140
Khan, Ustad Bade Ghulam Ali, 149
Khan, Ustad Faiyaz, 140
Khan, Ustad Hafiz Ali, 140, 143, 144
Khan, Ustad Ishtiaq Hussain, 144
Khan, Ustad Jafar Hussain of Badaun, 14
Khan, Ustad Jamiruddin, 57
Khan, Ustad Mushtaq Hussain, 144, 150–158
Khan, Ustad Nasir Aminuddin, 144
Khan, Ustad Nasir Moizuddin, 56
Khan, Ustad Vilayat Husain, 140, 144, 149
Khanqah-e-Niazia, 153
Kipling, Rudyard, 78
kothas, 126
Kumar Sambhav, 159

L

labh-e-mashooqa, 121
Lakhia, Kumudini, 145
Liberation War, 54
Lily Cottage, 41–42, 44
Linlithgow, Lord, 127
Lucknow, 17, 83, 87, 93, 95, 101, 117–125

M

Maharaj, Guru Acchan, 140
Maharaj, Guru Shambhu, 144
Maharani Girls High School, 49
Martin Luther of India, *see* Sen, Keshub Chandra
Marx, Karl, 40
Mayurbhanj, 16, 30, 47–48, 53
mehfils, 175
Mishra, Ram Prasad, 57
Miyan, Aziz, 153–156
Montagu-Chelmsford Reforms, 115
Mughal Empire, 20–21, 117, 120
mujras, 122, 123
murabba, 121
Murshidabad, 26
Muslim League, 128
mutanjan, 121

N

Naba Bidhan, 34
nagarakirtana, 39
Narayan, Shovana, 61, 145, 160,
Native Manager of the Hindoostanee Press, 29
Native Secretary of the Asiatic Society, 29–30
Nat Mandir, 27
Nawab Mir Qasim, 22
Nawab of Awadh, 22
Nawab of Bengal, 22, 25. *See* Siraj-ud-Daulah
nazakat, 120
Niazi Silsila, 153
Nizam of Hyderabad, 80, 113

O

Omar Khayyam, 61–62
Osbourne, W. G., 89

P

Paigham, 60
Palashi. *See* Battle of Plassey
Prasada Bhawan, 122
Prasada, Kanwar Jwala, 85
Prasad, Guru Sundar, 144
Presidency College, 32
Prodeep, Sen, 51
Punjab, 15–16, 64, 74–77, 80–84, 116, 174
Pusa Road, 142–150

R

Raag Rang 1, 164–169
Raag Rang 2, 172–178
Raja-i-Rajgan, 83
Rajanagar, 100–104
Rajkumar, Guru Senarik, 55
Raj Nartaki, 15, 59
Ramakrishna, Shri, 43–44
Rampur, 160–164
Rampur-Sahaswan gharana, 14
Rao, Bhaiyasahib Ganpat, 55
Rao, C.B., 133
Rao, Maya, 145
Rao, Sharda, 133–135
Roy, Benita, 16, 52–54

Roy, Chakma Raja Nalinaksha, 53
Roy, Raja Ram Mohan, 32–35
Roy, Tridiv, 53

S

Sadharan Brahmo Samaj, 34
Sangeet Natak Akademi, 134, 141, 153, 166, 174
sankirtana, 39
Sanskrit College, 30
Sarkar, Hemlata, 49
Sarkar, Ratan, 24
Sen, Keshub Chandra, 16, 28, 33, 193
  of Brahmo Samaj, 35–37
  children, 45–50
  death, 44–45
  education for women, 34
  Lily Cottage, purchase of, 41–42
Sen, Nirmala, 51–52, 62, 65
Sen, Ram Kamal, 23, 28–34
  Asiatic Society, 31–32
  birth, 29
  contributions, 29–30
  education, interest in, 30
Sen, Saral, 50–52
Shah Alam II, 22–23, 118
Shankar, Pandit Ravi, 140
Shankar Parvati, 60
Sharma, Uma, 145, 154, 160, 175, 178, 181
Shlokasangraha, 39
shringar, 122
Simla
  arrival in, 74
  British in, 78
  growth of, 75–76
  journey to, 68–69
Simla Conference, 128
Simla Manifesto, 89
Singh, Chandrajit, 186–187
Singh, Kanwar Ripjit, 16, 69–70, 72, 81, 87
Singh, Kanwar Suchet, 70–71, 81, 82, 95, 117
Singh, Raja Charanjit, 69, 70–72, 81, 83–84, 169–172
Singh, Raja Nihal, 82
Singh, Raja Randhir, 82
Singh, Rajkumar Ajit, 72
Singh, Rajkumar Sarabjit, 72
Singh, Rani Nina Ripjit, 15, 65–135
Singh, Ranjit Maharaja, 76
Singh, Rena Ripjit, 15, 87, 93, 130, 147
Siraj-ud-Daulah, 22, 25
Snowdon complex, 80
Street Dancer, 62
Sulabh Samachar, 40
Summerhill, 70, 73
Sutanuti, 21
Sutlej Valley, 74

T

Tagore, Debendranath, 35–36
Tagore, Rabindranath, 15, 16, 33, 35, 53, 59, 61, 86
taluqdars, 83, 120–121
Taqi, Hazrat Shah Mohammed. *See* Miyan, Aziz
Tarikh-e-Thumri, 169
tawaifs, 56, 123, 124, 126, 139, 161
Thakur Dhalan, 27
Theravada Buddhism, 53
thumri, 13–14, 52, 56–57, 142, 150, 189–191
trompe l'oeils, 121

V

Versailles, 83
Viceregal Lodge, 78, 80
Viceroy's Executive Council, 69, 128
Viceroy's House, 104, 110, 114, 116
Vidyasagar, Ishwarchandra, 33
Vishkanya, 60
Vivekananda, 43–44

W

Wavell, Lord, 127–128
Western education, 32
Wilson, Horace H., 29
World War I, 113
World War II, 74, 127

Z

Zamani, Begum Rafat, 163–164
Zamindari system, 120
zamindars, 21, 85, 103, 109, 120, 144